Daddies
and
Daughters

CARMEN RENEE BERRY
AND LYNN BARRINGTON

A Fireside Book
Published by Simon & Schuster

FIRESIDE
Rockefeller Center
1230 Avenue of the Americas
New York, NY 10020

First Fireside Edition 1999

FIRESIDE and colophon are registered trademarks
of Simon & Schuster Inc.

Manufactured in the United States of America

3   5   7   9   10   8   6   4   2

**The Library of Congress has cataloged the
Simon & Schuster edition as follows:**

Berry, Carmen Renee.
Daddies and daughters / Carmen Renee Berry and
Lynn Barrington.
p.   cm.
1. Fathers and daughters — United States.   2. Parent and child —
United States.   3. Parenting — United States.   I. Barrington,
Lynn.   II. Title.
HQ755.85.B478   1998
306.874′2 — dc21
98-17972
CIP

ISBN 0-684-84992-5
ISBN 0-684-84993-3 (Pbk)

Acknowledgments

We are grateful to all the dads and daughters, of all ages, backgrounds, and races, who so graciously and candidly shared their stories with us. Without you, this book would never have been born.

For believing in us, we thank the "overlooked" parent of this project, our mothers Mary Lynn Bowden and Mary Ellen Berry. We love you both with all our hearts.

Lynn wants to especially honor her brothers Joe and Bill and their sweet families: you will always be the core part of who I become. Lynn also gives special thanks to the Kear family: Brad, for boundless love, Spock insights and acceptance through the years; Lisa, for sharing in the "sisterhood"; Chelsea, for letting me be her "girl-friend," and then her aunt; Evan and Claire, my darling babies who are a big six years old now, for being there to love and hold. In addition, Lynn is grateful to Mark Lowry, for believing in me when others didn't and for always being there via his telecommunication toys; to Jm J Bullock, who has shared life's ups and downs; to Marlice and John, who taught me the art of being okay to embrace what I want out of life, even after I botch things (I'm sorry, John); to Debby Halverson Markey, my soulmate, thanks for believing and calling out the best in me, Fred Markey . . . Um . . . in him; special thanks to Karla York for her continual love; thanks go to

Elaine Hill and Mark Ferber for every moment and second with you at the Bowl or anyplace else; to my many Los Angeles and Nashville friends — you know who you are — Lynn is grateful for your continued belief and prayers to make this project happen; and to Dr. Terry Lanford and Dr. Joe Pachorek — finally I found physicians who actually took the time to listen and then help . . . what a blessing you are! Lynn also wants to especially thank Mary Rotzein for her time and wise thoughts given in the course of this book; and thanks go to the Mauldin family — Tiffani, Melissa, Henry, Chad, Abigail, Amanda, and huggable Trey for adding spice and flare to my life; Jim and Joy Dawson, for teaching me to pray first; John and Julie Dawson, for loving my guy while he didn't know me. Lynn is also grateful to the Bledsoe family; Darrell, for being the most awesome and creative partner a person could dream of; Beverly — I watch and learn the "art of being gracious" from you; Laura and Amanda — your lives honor your dad. Lynn would like to thank all her new Texas friends, John, Foster, Hannah, Heather Devron, Dr. Farley Brown, and Pastor Ed Williams, and her special golfing buddies, Donna and Michael Williams. Lastly, Lynn would like to thank her two nieces, Lavenia and Toni Bowden. Girls, I am so proud of both of you and I never would have made it through these last few months without your love and support.

Carmen extends her gratitude to her friends, not only for the support given during the writing of this book, but for the immeasurable love, prayers, and practical assistance given during her dad's recent accident and subsequent death: to Cathy and Bob, for daily care and being a limitless source of needed information; to Tamara Traeder, for jumping on a plane and organizing the chaos; to Roy Carlisle, for jumping on the plane with her and being in ICU during the thick of things; to Pat Luehrs, for regularly visiting the hospital without being asked; to Irene Flores, who kept her laughing through the tears; to Joel Miller, who shared his personal support and professional wisdom; to Gail Walker, who knows what it's like to be an only child in such circumstances; to Bob Myers, who sent around the "help out the Berrys" sign-up sheet; to Rene Chansler, who lifted spirits with oodles of humorous e-mails; to Dr. Paul Roberts, who was willing to do therapy by phone on the days that were too overwhelming; and to those who visited the hospital, left supportive phone messages and e-mails, and sent cards: Mark Baker, Rick Fraser, Susan Latta, Carolyn Braddock, Bobette Buster, Barbara Berry, Cheryl Carole, Beverly Futer, Heidi Kahlstorf, Karen Lee-Thorp, Kathy Hoffman, Leslie Hoffman, Jim Kermath, Crystal Nash, Scott Brick, Connie and Trevor, Jody Kranz, Renee Lonner, Joan Rosenberg, Joe and Sheila Palocios, Paul and Paula Reza, Laura Robinson, Cory and Claudia Saldana, Carolyn Thacker, Dale Wolery, Dale Ryan and Dan Psaute.

For keeping our papers straight, our phone calls returned, and generally saving our lives, we thank our assistants Marianne Croonquist, Terry Dixon and Kristi

Lovette. Without these women, we'd never have made deadline.

We give an enthusiastic round of applause for our agent, Kathy Yanni of Alive Communications, for proving that business can be conducted with integrity, intelligence, and unfailing wit. We love you! At Simon & Schuster, we thank David Rosenthal, Annik LaFarge, John Mooney, Jennifer Engels, and Rachel Burd. Special thanks go to our editor, Betsy Herman, for believing in this project with passion and pizzazz. We are also most grateful to Matthew Walker, for hounding us, cajoling us, e-mailing us, and forgiving us throughout the creation of this manuscript.

We want to give special acknowledgment to the dynamic publicity team at JMPR & Associates, Inc., in New York City. On a moment's notice, they came on board with their incredible energy and, along with Simon & Schuster, pushed us to number 12 on the Barnes & Noble Top 100 list and to number 1 on the Family and Relationships list. Those who said it couldn't be done do not know the power of Julie McQuain! Thank you all.

Dedicated to Our Dads
Jeff Benney Bowden
and, in dearest memory,
Dr. David A. Berry

Contents

It's a Girl!

Having a daughter was like falling in love,
like meeting God.

—DAVID, ALEXANDRA'S FATHER

Make Room for Daddy

Arthur always has his arms around [his daughter] Camera. When he talked about her, his face would light up like stars in the sky. He showed more feeling for his daughter than I had seen him show his whole life.

— HARACE ASHE, UNCLE OF ARTHUR ASHE

In days of yore, fathers-to-be were banished to pace anxiously around hospital maternity wards waiting to find out if "it" was a girl or a boy, while their wives gave birth behind closed doors. The first time some new daddies laid eyes on their newly born daughters might have been through the thick glass window overlooking a nursery full of cribs and crying infants. Lynn, one of the authors, related how her father reacted to hearing the words "It's a girl!":

"Back then fathers weren't allowed in the delivery room, and since they didn't have sonograms, the tension mounted as the time came for me to show my little face. The doctor came out to tell my aunt Peggy and my daddy, who was keeping the waiting room vigil alive with stories of his escapades in the oil field. When the news came that I was a girl, my aunt said my daddy started handing out cigars and then headed down to my mom's room. She said she'd never forget seeing him click his heels, two times like Fred Astaire, as he sauntered off to see his brand-new little baby girl. Both my mom and my aunt had never seen or heard of him doing that before, or since. He was a happy guy that day."

With today's technological changes, fathers can now catch the first glimpse of their daughters on a screen, usually with the help of medical personnel who can make sense of the wavering black-and-white images. And because of this technology, fathers do not have to wait nine months to know the gender of their child-to-be.

Michael, a first-time father, told us that the first time he saw his daughter was when his wife had an ultrasound: "The doctor was an old-fashioned kind of doctor and he didn't volunteer telling us whether she was a boy or a girl. Since I couldn't tell the baby's gender from looking at the screen, I realized one of us would have to ask him. But I guess I'm old-fashioned too. I wanted to be told. So I looked at it, and thinking I knew more than I did, I decided to myself the baby was a boy.

"Part of my problem was that I prided myself on my hunches. In fact, I knew my wife was pregnant before she did! I told her I thought she was pregnant and she laughed, 'No, I'm not. I would know if I were pregnant.' But sure enough, she was, so I was pretty sure of myself when I decided we were having a boy."

Michael spent several months secure in his "hunch." When he was away on a business trip in Ireland, he visited a church and, he told us, "the perfect name just came to me. We'll name him Christian! I thought, it's got to be an omen." Right up until the moment of birth, Michael was sure he was about to have a son.

Finally, he and his wife were in the delivery room. He described the birth to us. "I was my wife's Lamaze coach. Well, actually I was more like a cheerleader, since I didn't really do anything except cheer her on, and say things like, 'Go girl. Let me know when you need some drugs!'

"In between my stints as cheerleader, I told everyone I was sure it was a boy. I told the doctor, the nurses, everyone who walked into the delivery room. And then the nurse said to me, 'It's a girl.' I look at the doctor and say, 'Yeah, right, you're lying to me.' I see the umbilical cord between her legs, and I'm thinking, 'He's not well hung.' The doctor said, 'Check that out. It's a girl,' and my jaw dropped. I was so off base that we hadn't even discussed a name if it turned out to be a girl.

"And then it hit me. We could call her Misha, which means Michael in Russian. When I was a boy, I was called Misha by my family, but I always thought it sounded like a girl's name. So, we called her Misha. I remember how it felt when I held her for the first time, and there was this nurse who said, in this sarcastic voice, 'Do you want to hold your child even though she's a girl?'

"I took her in my arms, feeling sorry for myself, and then I looked into her face. My heart melted, and I told her, 'I'm your daddy. I'll take care of you. I'll always be there for you.' And, so far, I've kept that promise."

David, another first-time father, also met his daughter-to-be via ultrasound and yet wanted to wait until the birth to find out the gender of his newborn. "It was weird to see my child for the first time through this technology," he told us. "The baby was in black and white, like seeing a plane in a storm on radar. The blip was there, but it wasn't fully recognizable, not like any baby picture I was used to seeing. Her eyes were open, like bright lights. But I had no idea if she were a she or a he.

"Even though they had the gender results, we wanted to find out the old-fashioned way. It was pretty ridiculous, really. We were at a supertechno hospital, getting all these fancy tests, and we wanted to wait to find out. My sister was really upset with us because she wanted to know what color to buy."

Not everyone chooses to be "old-fashioned" and may find out the baby's gender before the birth. Regardless of when a father finds out he's got a daughter, all of the fathers we talked to said that when they held their daughters in their arms for the first time, something amazing happened to them. Alan, who had one son before his two daughters were born, told us about preparing for their births: "We went to the Lamaze classes and, to be truthful, I was relatively worthless. If I had been down there with a catcher's mitt, I think I would have been more useful. I spent most of my time in the southern half yelling things up to my wife like, 'C'mon, you're doing great, just keep breathing, it's good for go down here.'

"When my son was born, he had the cord wrapped

around his neck and he was blue. We were so frightened that he was going to die. It took three of them to work on him for about thirty seconds before he started crying. When the doctor said, 'It's a boy,' I got this proud feeling, like, 'hey, Dude, I made a boy!' But there's a different feeling when you make a son, versus when a daughter is born. A completely different feeling. Instead of 'hey, Dude,' it's like, 'ohhhhh, I get to be this protector, this provider, this warm, loving person.' With my son I thought, this is someone I can play catch with, someone who will change my tires when I get older. But when both girls were born, there was a real sense of fatherly responsibility to take care of these new lives."

Besides, with a sense of responsibility and protectiveness, dads can feel like a duck out of water at the thought of raising a daughter. Being males themselves, fathers have a more natural understanding of what a baby boy needs. But females, whether women or infants, can be a bit mysterious to men. Some fathers can feel awkward or even left out as the mother-daughter bond develops. David told us how he "made room for himself" in the life of his daughter. He said, "I got to cut the cord, which is a little like cutting through whale blubber, sort of thick and gristly. Cutting the cord was more than just a medical procedure for me. There was a mystical side of it. I stood between her and her mother and cut her from her mother. In a real sense I said to my daughter, 'Okay kid, I'm separating you. It's you and me and her. It's the three of us.'

17

"I was so grateful that my first child was a girl that I could not stop the tears. I don't know if I would have felt as free with my tenderness and affection if I'd had a son. I felt the freedom to exalt over her. I've been with friends' children and I've found that little boys like nurturing too. Now having had her, if our next child is a little boy, I know I'll be able to flood over him like I have over a daughter. I'm so glad she was my first."

Vito echoed David's sentiment about having a baby girl. "The first six months I was saying I wanted a baby boy," he told us. "But halfway through my wife's pregnancy something came over me and I started rooting for a girl. My wife thought I was being nice, hedging against being disappointed at not having a boy. But that wasn't the truth. I loved having a girl. I told my friend, who has a twenty-two-month-old baby boy, 'I don't know what it feels like to have a son, but the feeling of having a girl is the best feeling I will probably ever have in life. Her lovingness is overwhelming to me.'"

Regardless of the sex of the newborn, the experience of sharing in the birth can be unforgettable, if not spiritual. Gary told us about how grateful he was to be a father in a day and age when he was allowed to participate rather than be sent off to some room to pace and wait. "At first we were just hanging around waiting, not knowing what to expect, because this was our first child," he recalled. "The doctor came in, checked my wife, and then told me to get scrubbed up because he could tell by the contractions that things were moving along. So I went in and scrubbed up, using a special kind of soap and scrubbers. By the time I got back, they were whisking her down the hallway to the delivery room. Everything was moving really fast. I don't know if they had waited too long, or that my wife was moving along faster than they expected, but I remember so vividly rushing right beside them, at the head of the table, hearing them tell her, 'Don't push, don't push.' While we were still in the hallway, I could see Carrie Ann's head crowning.

"I was filled with a sense of amazement. For nine months we had been anticipating this moment, and yet until you're there, you can't really envision what it's like until it's happening. So when I saw this fuzzy, mucous-laden-looking item appearing, I thought, 'Oh, my God, that's a real life right there!' It's a fulfillment of a very long awaited happening, the feeling that you had some part of this creation. It's a very gratifying moment."

That moment is the beginning of hundreds of thousands of special moments that form the daddy-daughter bond. As the story of each unique relationship unfolds, these experiences have the power to change forever the way dad or daughter looks at life. But the moment of birth has primal significance. Even though the mother has had nine months to bond with her daughter, the father is the one who has the first opportunity to welcome his daughter into the world the second she arrives. She may have been in her mother's womb, but she's now in her father's arms.

When a daughter first meets her daddy, a special relationship begins that will shape and mold them both from that moment forward. She makes room in her heart for the first significant man in her life — and becomes Daddy's little girl.

You Showed Up Early

The first time I saw my baby girl, she was a peach color.
She might have seemed like an ugly baby to some,
but to me she was absolutely beautiful.

— ERIC, BLAIR'S FATHER

When soon-to-be moms and dads imagine the arrival of their new baby, most envision a full-term pregnancy and the birth of a healthy infant ready to deal with life outside the womb. Plans are made around the expected due date, with dads having ample time to prepare mentally (and even practice driving to the hospital if need be) for the big event. For some fathers, however, the time is cut short abruptly when they hear the words "honey, it's time" and find themselves engaged in a life-and-death struggle that is beyond anything they or their wives could have anticipated.

Brad and Lisa did not know ahead of time they were going to become parents of preemies. They did know, however, that Lisa was going to give birth to twins. Brad recalled, "The doctor first told us something was amiss, and we thought we might have a baby with Down's syndrome. So Lisa had an amniocentesis. That's when we found out that she was carrying both a boy and a girl.

"There's always the risk of giving birth prematurely with twins, but we had no idea what we were really in for. At thirty weeks, Lisa went into labor and I rushed

21

her to the hospital. They attached a monitor to her to gauge the severity of her contractions, hoping to delay birth as long as possible. Each day the babies stayed inside the womb was like a week of development. After she had been in labor for two days, she was absolutely miserable, complaining that the contractions were really strong.

"What we, and the hospital staff, didn't know was that the monitor was broken. The nurse said, 'Lisa, the monitor says you are at only a level two.' Lisa, in no uncertain terms, let her know this had to be more than a level two, so the nurse checked and found her dilated at ten centimeters! That meant it was time to hit the road to the delivery room.

"Everything happened very quickly after that. They called the doctors and rushed her into surgery immediately because they thought Claire's head was crowning. It turned out to be her bottom, so they decided to do a cesarean. When the doctor pulled out Claire, she looked like a little bird who had fallen out of the nest. Her skin was very translucent and she had a big, huge black eye. They went to work immediately on her, and within two or three minutes she and her brother were both yanked out and taken to the neonatal room.

"Lisa didn't get to see Evan and Claire when they first came into the world. I saw them because I got to watch the whole thing. Lisa had been given morphine, and I remember she had the biggest smile on her face. She didn't have the ability to know how sick they were. She knew they were early, but she didn't know they were really ill. So I went into the neonatal room, where they were both strapped down to the warmers. Evan was a few ounces larger, but Claire was so small, even a preemie diaper would not fit her. They just got pieces of gauze and wrapped it around her little midsection because that's how small she was. It was scary."

With premature births, the babies are not out of the woods just because they are out of the womb. Brad described the challenges that awaited his tiny daughter. "Claire had fluid around her heart when she was born. The doctors needed to extract the fluid because it might cause pressure on the heart. They had to send away for the smallest needle that was ever manufactured. Even though the doctors didn't say 'she'll probably die,' we knew her chances were slim because they wouldn't give us any encouragement whatsoever. It was very hard on me."

Fortunately for Brad and Lisa, Claire survived the procedure and eventually gained in strength and weight. Evan came home in six weeks, and, after eight weeks, Claire too was released to go home. Once again, they were confronted with the unexpected. Brad recalled, "The day we brought her home she weighed three pounds three ounces; none of the baby clothes we'd been given were small enough, so we pulled some clothes off her older sister's dolls and put those on her."

Expecting the unexpected is much of what one feels with a premature birth. One father told us how his life was turned upside down one afternoon when he learned that his wife went into labor after only four months of pregnancy. Doug said, "My wife, Debby, is a neonatal nurse and was working at the hospital when she went into preterm labor. Some of the other nurses took matters into their own hands, grabbed my wife by the arm, and 'escorted' her to a high-risk obstetrician. After the ultrasound revealed that the placenta was pulling away from the wall of the uterus, she was told she had to stay in bed from week sixteen to thirty-three to save the baby.

"Of course, this threw our lives into turmoil. Debby decided to stay at her parents' home so she could be cared for around-the-clock. I was either at home alone, or forced to move my life to her parents' home. That was tough not only on our relationship, but just on my mental well-being as a man. I decided the only thing I could do was take it one day at a time. People would ask constantly, 'How can you go through this?' When you are in the situation, you don't have a choice."

Not only was their living situation altered dramatically, but also any sense of what to expect for the duration of the pregnancy, and most certainly at the birth. Doug explained, "I was scared, not knowing what was going to happen next. We knew the baby would be born prematurely, so she would only be around three or four pounds. But then, again, you never know. All the doctors can do is give you their best guess, and certainly no guarantees. One thing working in our favor was that the premature labor had tipped us off that something was amiss. We were better prepared than we would have been if Debby had suddenly gone into labor at thirty-three weeks.

"After my wife was in labor about twenty-four hours, the baby's heart rate decelerated when the contractions began compressing the umbilical cord, which was only about twelve inches long, substantially shorter than normal. Even though I'd had months to prepare, I was still surprised at how tiny Tiffany was, and yet fully formed. After a few days with oxygen, she was soon breathing on her own and didn't have to have any invasive procedures. Even still, we didn't get to hold her for several days. The first time I held her, she seemed so small, all wrapped up in blankets. She was three pounds — holding her was like holding not much of anything."

Full-term babies often go home a day or two after birth. Not so with preemies. Many stay in the hospital for weeks as their bodies continue to grow, as they would have had they stayed in the womb full-term. Tiffany was fortunate in that her mother was a neonatal nurse so the doctor was willing to let her go home after twelve days. Whenever Tiffany ran into any kind of trouble, her mother was there to care for her. Doug told us, "Debby was still in pain from childbirth, yet she was right there, taking care of Tiffany. And that's why Tiffany's been such a healthy little girl."

Tiffany was Doug and Debby's first of three — all born prematurely. After Tiffany, Debby gave birth to a boy, who overcame the challenges of a premature birth, and then to their third child, a little girl named Amanda. Amanda suffered a variety of physical problems. Doug told us, "As soon as Debby found out she was pregnant again, the doctor sent her to bed. After twenty weeks of bed rest, Amanda was born at one pound, twelve ounces.

"Even though at first she breathed on her own, she developed heart problems. During her first of her many surgeries, her laryngeal nerve was severed, which controls her vocal cords. As a result, one of her vocal cords is completely paralyzed and the other is partially paralyzed and only thirty percent functional, and she has to have a tracheostomy to breathe and has to wear a trach collar now. Amanda has now been through sixteen surgeries. This, of course, doesn't count the numerous other procedures she's endured. No one thought she would come through all of this. At one point the doctors told us, 'It's now up to God, as we can't do anything more.' And yet, she still survived."

Doug spoke of his daughter with admiration, if not awe: "Amanda will not give up. She has adapted to the fourteen medications, the oxygen, the ventilator, pulse oscillator, apnea monitor, and the trach collar. She gets up in the morning and puts her trach collar on, has breakfast, and starts playing as she drags her fifty-foot oxygen tube around with her. We put a trach collar on one of her dolls, and when Amanda goes through certain procedures, her 'baby' goes through it, too. She's an amazing one."

Fathers like Doug of children born prematurely gain

a sense of respect for these daughters for overcoming such immense challenges while being so very, very small. When we asked Brad how he thinks being born prematurely impacted his daughter Claire, he told us, "She didn't bond to us at first. I remember her laying on her side in that glass enclosure, watching everything that went on in the NICU. She never cried. She never acted like she wanted someone to hold her. To this day she remains somewhat aloof and very independent. She started out life as a fighter, and that quality has already served her well in life."

These early arrivers have to fight extra hard to survive, and their daddies often fight right alongside them. Because of this shared struggle, a bond of mutual respect and admiration can form between them. While all fathers may delight when their daughters take their first step, dads of preemies celebrate all the more since they realize the vast distance their daughters had to travel. They are blessed to watch their little daughters do what used to be the impossible.

Your Mother Was Awesome

During our first birth, I just about passed out when they did the cesarean, if that tells you anything. I hung in there, but it was her body that had to live through it.

— BILL, MEGHANN'S FATHER

When a woman gives birth, a marvelous transformation takes place before her husband's eyes, transforming her from a mere female into a *mother*. We spoke with several fathers who were amazed — and impressed — by the strength and stamina their wives exhibited, power that these men didn't know their wives had within them.

Doug told us that he was impressed with what his wife *didn't* do during her pregnancies. He said, "She had to stay in bed for all three of our children. Counting all three children, she stayed in bed well over a year and four months.

"I can't even imagine what it was like to have to lay there day after day. I got to get up and go to work every day, play golf, or whatever I wanted to do while she was down and out of action. I spent a lot of time with her, so I have a little idea of what it was like. Nevertheless, she was the one who had to stay there around-the-clock. I admire her so much, because she's the one who actually did it!"

Another father told us that he had to reevaluate his perception of his wife when she went into labor. David told us, "While I expected the birth process to be emotional, I did not expect Sophia to respond like she did. Prior to this event, I had experienced her as someone volatile in her emotions, squeamish, and not able to deal well with pain. However, from the time she broke her water, Sophia became Earth Mother. This very able, very strong person burst out of her that I'd never seen before.

"At the hospital, she and I sat together for several hours, talking about her growing up in Beirut. She began to identify very strongly with women in the Third World. They didn't go to hospitals there. The process was very natural. She told me about women in the village near where she grew up; when they gave birth, they squatted down to deliver.

"Later, she walked the hospital halls with her girl-friends, and when a contraction would come, she'd be in midsentence and simply stop talking for a moment. Then she'd pull herself up and pick up the conversation where she had left off. I was very impressed. I felt very small in the face of this towering strength I'd never met before. She was amazing."

Some women show their more amazing qualities when something goes awry with the birth process and they are presented with an extra challenge. Roy spoke of Chris, the mother of his two daughters, with tenderness and respect: "When Erica, our first child, was born, we were all a little ignorant about the whole thing. We decided to have a home delivery, so we chose a male midwife, a doctor who was famous for delivering home births.

"Chris's water broke on Friday night. We called the

doctor, who told us to keep him up-to-date on the timing of the contractions. We did, and she started to go into hard labor after six or seven hours. He came by early Saturday morning, but told us she was not dilated fully, so he left, telling us to keep him posted.

"We spent all day Saturday doing breathing exercises, while Chris was having strong labor contractions. She never got to sleep, although I snuck in a little nap. She was a trouper. After a nurse's aide, Debbie, came by and checked Chris, finding that she had dilated to nine centimeters, she immediately contacted the doctor. He wanted to wait until she was fully dilated at ten centimeters. What we didn't know was that Chris's body doesn't dilate that far, ever.

"By now, it's early Sunday morning. She's in serious labor. She's exhausted. The doctor came over and realized this was all we were going to get. So Debbie and I got on either side, and when Chris had a contraction, we had to push the baby down the birth canal because she was so tired she didn't have the strength to push the baby through a nine-centimeter opening. Finally, the midwife massaged the baby out, and Erica was born a little after nine A.M. on Sunday morning.

"After the baby was born, I went around the little complex where we lived and explained to the neighbors what all the commotion had been for two days. We lived in a little courtyard, and everyone knew something was going on. By eleven A.M. we had thirty people in the house to celebrate. Through the whole thing, Chris was

30

amazing. I just don't even know how to say it. She was superwoman. I wouldn't have lasted that long.

"Since we knew this about Chris, our second daughter was born in about five hours. We just told the doctor not to wait after she dilated to nine centimeters. We could have shortened the first delivery by about thirty-five hours had we known!"

Facing the unknown on the delivery table can be the perfect place for a man to gain new respect for his wife. Brad remembers when the doctors suddenly decided to perform a cesarean to deliver the twins his wife, Lisa, was carrying. He said, "Normally the husband would have to be out of the way, but it was all moving so quickly, they didn't worry about me. I saw them literally slice open her stomach. I went into intellectual mode and became Spock from *Star Trek*. 'The slice has been made, Captain!' I was into the whole thing in a scientific, non-emotional, logical sort of way.

"Lisa had ahold of my hand, and she couldn't feel the pain of the incision, but could feel the tugging and the pressure. She looked up at me, and her eyes were as big as saucers, saying, 'I can't believe it!' The only other sign of nervousness I noticed were her feet wriggling at the other end of the table.

"To be honest with you, I felt pretty numb through the process, because it all happened within a matter of ten minutes. I was so impressed with what she had just been through. I told her that I would worship at her feet for the rest of my life for doing this so we could have a family. Of course I haven't, but I do admire what Lisa had to go through to have our little girl and boy. I certainly don't think I am capable of it!" (And any woman who has given birth would most likely agree.)

Many men stand amazed at what their wives go through to give them a child. There could be no father-daughter bond to celebrate if it were not for the mothers. Roy summed up what many fathers felt with the words "My wife was a trouper." It comes down to that.

Anxious Moments

My father told me that from the beginning, I've taught him to appreciate life and to be thankful for what he has.

— CYNTHIA, IVAN'S DAUGHTER

Giving birth, even with all the modern medical advances, has unavoidable risks to both mother and child. The father, who loves them both, is deeply affected by the "what ifs," the "chances are," and the "there might be a problem here."

Not only does current medical technology, at some point, fail to guarantee a smooth pregnancy and delivery, our ability to view inside the womb can create anxiety for the expectant parents. David told us, "Early in Sophia's pregnancy she had a blood test that indicated an elevated risk of a birth defect, Down's syndrome. The doctor recommended we have an amniocentesis. We had already decided that whatever 'hatched' we were going to love, but wanted to go through with the procedure in order to help us prepare.

"Before the procedure we were shown a tape explaining all the possibilities. As we watched the footage of Down's children we were both in tears because they were so beautiful. If the amnio revealed an extra chromosome, we were already very much in love with this child. Our biggest apprehension revolved around the risks of the test itself. We knew that there was a chance of premature labor, so it was a scary time. We were so relieved that Sophia made it through the test without losing the baby. And we were finally able to relax once the test results came back saying nothing was wrong."

David and Sophia may have breathed a sigh of relief once this initial challenge ended, but their anxious moments were not quite over. David's next challenge was dealing with a hospital whose staff and facilities were less than acceptable. The day of delivery, the hot water system at the hospital went out. He recalled, "I was so angry at the hospital for not having hot water. We had planned to have Sophia rest in a warm bath prior to delivery with my rubbing her back. I really looked forward to being a part of the birth in this way. When all we had was cold water, I was frustrated and angry. When I expressed my feelings, our male nurse was a little callous and a little unfeeling. I wanted to deck him a couple of times, but I thought that might be counterproductive. I didn't want my daughter's birth and my arrest on the same day!"

The final anxious moment was not far away, as Sophia was moved into the delivery room and the heart monitor began to read the baby's heartbeat. "Every time my wife had a contraction," David told us, "the baby's heart rate dropped dramatically or disappeared. We found out later that the umbilical cord had been wrapped around her arms and chest, so every time Sophia squeezed, it would squeeze her chest, pulling her away from the monitor, so it appeared that her heartbeat was changing.

"They called out the crisis SWAT team, and they put

what is called a 'scalp clip' into her head. The term 'clip' is reassuring, but in reality it's a screw, like what's in a ballpoint pen, that is stuck into her scalp and monitors her heartbeat. Because of this 'clip' she had a sore on her scalp for more than a year. But the good news was that our fears during the delivery were replaced by the thrill of having a healthy baby girl."

Some couples experience a relatively "easy" pregnancy and birth, but are confronted with their anxious moments after the baby has safely made it into the world. Roy, father of two college-age girls, told us about a near-fatal mistake he made while assisting in the birth of his second daughter, Vanessa: "I was assisting the doctor in giving birth and, having done this once before with my elder daughter, I thought I was a birthing expert. Prior to cutting the umbilical cord, I began to stroke the cord, moving the blood in the direction of the baby, or at least that's what I thought. In a calm voice, the doctor said, 'Roy, it usually works better if the baby has blood to live. So you might want to stroke that the other direction.' We all cracked up. I quickly reversed directions, and she was fine. But I learned a big lesson in humility that day."

Some babies are born strong and healthy, only for the parents to find out after birth that all things are not quite as positive as they had thought. Cynthia told us about the emotional pain her parents suffered when, soon after her birth, they were told that she might be blind: "My folks told me my mom was devastated and cried for three days. My dad was also struggling. On the third day after they received the news about my vision, my dad was driving to the hospital. All of a sudden he looked up at the clouds, wondering how he would describe them to me if I indeed couldn't see. He said it was as if his eyes really opened for the first time in his life. Clouds weren't just white blobs. They were soft billowy huge puffs of cotton. The grass wasn't just a blanket of green, but instead he noticed that it was thousands upon thousands of tiny individual blades. He looked at everything, taking in the world around him the rest of the way to the hospital. He's never stopped appreciating the gift of sight and the gift of life God's given him, even after they found out my eyesight was fine."

In Cynthia's case, the anxious moments were replaced with relief. Unfortunately, this is not always the case. After celebrating the birth of their daughter Misha, Michael and his wife were stunned to find out four months later that Misha was diagnosed with brain cancer. "She's beaten the odds to make it this far," he told us, "even though she's been considered terminal for years.

"Prior to her diagnosis, I was at work all the time, thinking this was the best way to provide for my family. I was working at the family business, out of town, eighty-five or ninety hours a week. I had a little cot there at the office, thinking I was being a good dad by providing financially.

"But when my daughter was diagnosed with cancer, I just quit. I just left it all to be there with her. She immediately had her first surgery, and about two or three weeks later she had a second surgery. Even though the surgery only lasted an hour, the doctor didn't come to talk to us for three hours. We found out later it was because the doctor was so upset at having to tell us it looked like our daughter would die. My wife asked, 'When will Misha be able to go home?' He said, 'Just take her home now and make her comfortable.'

"She's now been through three brain surgeries. They took out thirty percent of the tumor around her brain stem during the first surgery. But one month later, the tumor was five times bigger, the size of a half-dollar, so she had to have surgery again. She developed an extreme case of hydrocephalus and almost died.

"But against all the odds, Misha is now four and going strong. She has changed my life. I was just a very hot-headed, mean, angry, one-directional sort of man. Because I love my daughter, I've changed. In fact, I refer to my life in terms of before and after her diagnosis. She has given me the strength because of her courage. She is such a fighter.

"No doctor, *nobody* tells me that she's going to die, not even God. I refused to let our insurance dictate the doctor who operated on her. They wanted us to go to a guy who rarely did this kind of surgery. I went to the insurance company and threatened to go to the newspapers, or do whatever was necessary to get a qualified surgeon for my daughter.

"I banged my fists down, and, finally, I got my way, because five and a half hours later they said, here is a wonderful doctor who is renowned in his field. My wife had this intuitive confirmation and said, 'Give Misha to him.' It was the right choice, and he has successfully operated on Misha on a number of occasions."

Time after time dads have spoken of how they have had to fight for their babies when insurance companies, hospital staff, doctors, and administration have been less than sensitive in responding to their needs. Many fathers have gone to unbelievable lengths to make sure their little girl or boy got the best of care. But there comes a point when even the best of human effort falls short, and all anyone can do is pray.

Brian spoke of his little girl, Amanda, who put both of her parents through some very anxious moments after she was born: "She was born a very healthy little girl. But Joan and I were first-time parents and ran into what we thought at the time was a very unusual problem. Amanda was not getting enough nutrition from Joan's milk. So, a few weeks into the process, we noticed she was not growing like other babies her age. We went to the doctor and immediately he put Amanda in the hospital.

"We both couldn't believe we were in this situation. We had never heard of it, though it turns out not to be that uncommon. The nursing staff was always quite nice to us, but they didn't have much hope for Amanda. In fact, I later found out that babies who come in with Amanda's condition usually don't survive.

"Joan felt horrible that her milk was the cause of this

problem. She spent night and day with Amanda. When she wasn't with Amanda, she would spend her time in the hospital chapel praying for her daughter. As I prayed for Amanda, I felt God gave me a peace that she would live. I never doubted that peace. Even when we were not encouraged by the doctors or nurses, I trusted what I felt God had told me. It was a miracle that Amanda did live. Today, when you look at my beautiful daughter you would never know she walked near death's door. She certainly is one of the lights of my life."

While most soon-to-be dads would say their unborn children are important to them, many do not realize just how much these little ones mean to them until confronted with the possibility that something may be going awry. At the real threat of loss, illness, or disability, dads draw on inner determination and spirituality to protect and assist their daughters as they fight to survive. By joining forces, daddies and daughters confront the challenges. Whether it's a dad like Michael, who takes on the hospital bureaucracy, or a daughter like Amanda, fighting to keep the nutrition in her little body, it's life's anxious moments that pull the daddy and daughter relationship into a special place that cannot be touched or forgotten.

It Broke My Heart
to Miss Your Birth

*It takes time for the absent to assume their true shape
in our thoughts.*

—COLETTE

In the early morning hours of April 13, Miriam nudged her sleeping husband, Oliver, letting him know that their second child was about to be born. Oliver jumped into action, having been through this once before when their two-year-old son, Philip, was born. Even though this was in the days when dads did not go into the delivery rooms with their wives, Oliver was determined to be on hand, as close as possible, to witness his child's birth. He was all the more determined because he had missed the moment when Philip was born.

Cathy continued the story: "When my mother was in labor with my brother, Philip, my father was pacing in the waiting room as the sun came up. The nurse finally said, 'Go have breakfast. It's going to be a while before the birth.' So he went out for breakfast. When he got back, the nurse said, 'Oh, Dr. Smith, you missed it! You have a baby boy!'

"Two years later, my mother was in labor with me, once again in the early morning. My father started his pacing ritual, and the nurse said, 'It will take a long time. Go have breakfast.' So, he decided to go to the cafeteria.

When he came back he heard that I came very quickly and, once again, he missed the birth.

"When my sister, Lisa, was born, my mother had an unusually long labor. My father insisted he would be there for the birth, so he missed breakfast, lunch, and dinner. Finally, the nurse encouraged him to pick up something to eat. He ran out and grabbed a late dinner and, sure enough, when he got back, he found that he had another daughter who had been born while he was gone.

"When my mother was in labor with Bruce, my youngest sibling, my father crossed his arms and said, 'I'm not budging. No matter how long it takes, or how many meals I miss, I want to be in the waiting room when the baby is born!"

While the father in our next story wasn't able to be in the room when his daughter was born, he was able to hear his newborn utter her first cry. Debbie told us, "Months before my birth, my father announced in robust certainty that he couldn't wait to see his little red-headed baby girl. 'Ahhh, Dick,' his friends would say, 'you know, sometimes we don't always get what we want. Especially in *that* department!' He never blinked an eye. He was going to have a red-headed baby girl. And he continued, with fervor, to let his universe know.

" 'Dick . . . listen, your show of faith is truly remarkable. But have you considered the consequences if it's another boy? Or a brunette?' His colleagues were beginning to worry. My father never wavered.

"Pops heard me before he ever laid eyes on me. He was home sick with the chicken pox when my mother, Doris, went into labor. The doctor was a good friend and had made arrangements to have a phone placed in the delivery room. As soon as I slipped out of that soft womb, a nurse dialed the number, raised the receiver to the doctor's ear.

" 'Dick,' the doctor grinned, 'I want you to be the first to hear your darling red-headed daughter speak her mind.' Whack! My protesting outcry was unmistakable. Pops saw me about five days later. Still sick with the pox and still confined to home, he gazed through our dining room window. Just a lump of a head with a whisper of red down as hair met his loving gaze as Mom held me up in the idling car. Pop's universe heard about the reality of his red-headed baby girl days before he could actually cling to me, wrapped around my little finger."

Even though Cathy's and Debbie's fathers were able to hold their newborn children soon after their births, being there (even if "there" is in the waiting room) is part of being a father. Missing out on that moment can feel as though a part of being a father has been taken away from you, especially when the dad has anticipated the moment for nine months.

This was the case with Carmen's father, who missed her birth because the United States Navy and the Pacific Ocean stood in his way. Carmen recalled, "I remember first hearing this story when I was a little girl, sitting on my dad's lap. He'd get tears in his eyes and tell me about how he didn't get to see me until I was five months old. He was serving in the navy during the Korean conflict aboard a naval destroyer. When the time drew closer for my birth, he requested a leave, but it was denied. He spoke with everyone who thought they might be able to help, but in the end he was not allowed to leave the ship for my arrival.

"My mother and my grandmother drove to the hospital once labor started. In an unusually short labor (my mother once told me she had monthly cramps more severe), I was born at eight pounds six ounces. A very round baby!

"Five months later, my dad's ship docked in Long Beach, California, and he laid eyes on me for the first time. I've seen sixteen-millimeter home movies of our meeting, and it's quite a welcome. I'm all dressed up in a fancy, uncomfortable-looking dress, with a bonnet tied under my chin. Clearly I'm hot and annoyed at the entire situation, because all you can see of me is my open, wailing mouth as my poor father is trying to greet me! I'm sure I would have been thrilled to see him had I realized who he was. I suspect all I wanted was to get that pretty little bonnet off my head."

Military duty has stood between more than one dad and daughter, as Noilene told us about her birth in 1946. "Back in those days, my dad was transferred from one military base to another, all over the world, and family housing wasn't readily available. Consequently, my mother went to live with her parents. When my mom went into labor, my dad couldn't get leave from duty, so he missed my birth. To make matters a bit worse, I was born with the cord around my neck. I was blue and almost dead. My mother thought, 'Oh, no. He'll never see his daughter alive!' Suddenly, I started breathing and my skin tone changed to pink. So, I did make it to see my dad after all!"

The journey of fatherhood has many opportunities for heartbreak. Missing your child's birth, regardless of the reason, can mark the beginning of this journey with a note of sadness. The causes of absence mean nothing when you can't be where you desperately want to be.

Picking Your Name

Both legally and familiarly, as well as in my books,
I now have only one name, which is my own.

— COLETTE

What's in a name? that which we call a rose
By any other name would smell as sweet.

— SHAKESPEARE

Choosing your child's name is a once-in-a-lifetime decision. We seem unable to love someone or something without a name, and often those we love the dearest are given nicknames or pet names to capture their special meaning in our hearts. Some parents want to name their children after beloved family members, popular entertainers, or respected public, historic, or literary figures. Others search out names that endow the bearer with a particular meaning or mission, such as names that translate to "a refreshing spirit," "strong in battle," or "lighthearted." Even though most of the fathers we talked to had participated in this significant decision, we found there is no one right way to select a name.

For Pat and his wife, deciding on a name involved taking family tradition into account. He told us, "I am Catholic and my wife is Jewish. In the Jewish religion, it's not right to name a child after someone living. I wanted to name my child, in some way, after my dad, whose name is Ermino. Since his name starts with an E we looked for girls' names that began with that letter. That's how we decided on Emily."

Diane's parents took their time choosing a name for their newly born daughter. She told us the story about how she got her name: "Planning ahead is one of my father's main things. In the process, they were near a radio trying to come up with a name for me. Over the radio came this song 'Diane' with the lyrics, 'I see heaven when I look in your eyes, / Smile for me, my Diane.' They thought 'Wow! That's a great song.' They loved the song and the name. I think that's a pretty romantic way to pick my name."

Another unique way of selecting a name is by allowing older siblings to help in the decision. Michael told us that his daughter, Misha, saw her new sister, Anna, just twenty minutes after she was born. Misha took to Anna immediately, as if Anna were her baby. "We were thinking of naming her Janie, but when we asked Misha, she said, 'Anna's her name!' Misha liked the name Anna, and since she couldn't speak that well, Anna was a name she could pronounce. So we kept it. When we tell Anna how she got her name, we won't say it's because Misha could say it!"

Certain names come in and out of fashion, much like clothes or cars. Some parents in the sixties selected outlandish names in reaction to the "establishment." Most parents who want unique names for their daughters also try to choose a name that won't become an embarrassment to their child in later years. Having a unique name

46

may have its advantages, but it can also prove to be confusing to young children, as was the case with Carmen, one of the authors, who received her name due to her father's attraction to unusual names. She said, "My mother wanted to name me Victoria Renee, after two of her closest girlfriends. However, my dad suggested the name Carmen, a name that is rarely given to girls of Anglo heritage. Consequently, my name became Carmen Renee Berry.

Laughing, she admitted, "I love my name now. It is unique and that's a plus for me. I like a name that has Spanish, French, and English heritage. But when I was a little girl, no one I knew had the name Carmen. I took the name very literally, as if it were made up of two words, 'car' and 'men.' I remember thinking, 'Why did my parents name me *auto mechanic?* That's a weird name for a little girl!"

"Of course, when I was in high school, the name became an asset, because the name has a passionate, sexy connotation. I remember one day I walked into journalism class, and one of the boys had cut out a newspaper ad for a porno type movie called *Carmen Baby.* That was an image I didn't mind!"

As Carmen has found out, names chosen for a baby girl must last a lifetime and may seem easier to carry at certain ages of life than others. David and his wife, Sophia, put a great deal of effort into selecting a name for their daughter, Alexandra: "We chose her name deliberately. Alexandra means defendress, protector of her people. And she does. She sticks up for people. She's a pretty tough little nut herself. She doesn't like it when children are being hurt. We have a dream that she'll grow into her name.

"We didn't plan for this, but Alexandra has nicknamed herself 'Zandra.' She's still too young to get all those syllables in the right order. I think it's a great name, 'Zandra.'" David laughed, "We don't know if she'll choose to spell it with a 'z' or an 'x,' you know, 'Xandra.' Kind of sounds like *Xena*, the television show. There will be Xena, the Warrior Princess, and Xandra, the Defender! I can see it now!"

Alexandra isn't the only daughter in the world to rename herself. Lynn, the other author of this book, had three first names, being named after her father's mother, mother's mother, and her mother, the last of which was Lynn. She took Lynn as a first name once she was old enough to make her opinions known.

Not only did Lynn change her first name, she also changed her last. Her family name was hard to pronounce and she was forever correcting people. One night, with her girlfriend Kilte and her husband, she came up with Barrington. The next day her new name was on her AFTRA (American Federation of Television and Radio Artists) card! Her dad responded the first time he got a head shot (an eight-by-ten-inch picture used in the acting field) of Lynn with her new last name by cutting off the bottom inch that included the name before framing the picture. He said, "I don't have a daughter with the last name Barrington in my will!" Lynn showed him that she had retained the family name as her middle name on her driver's license, and peace was restored.

One father we talked to expressed concern over the nickname his daughter had been given by others outside the family. Doug, the father of eight-year-old Tiffany, told us, "Tiffany is very tiny. In fact, she's not even on the growth charts for her age. At forty-two inches tall and thirty-one pounds, most of her friends tower over her. In fact, they call her 'little Tiffany' and she goes along with it, seeming to enjoy it. I hope that she can always keep that positive attitude and it doesn't become a hindrance as she grows older."

Because names can carry symbolic power, what we are called, and certainly what we call ourselves, has great meaning. The changing of first or last names is a time when a daughter may express her individuality. And while dads have a say in what we are named originally, they can't protect us from names others might give us. Ultimately, only we, the daughters, have the power to decide which names we will discard and which we will carry.

Daddy-Daughter Bonding

As the father of a daughter, you start to glory in things
you never thought you'd care about.

— DAVID, ALEXANDRA'S FATHER

A man prides himself on his strength — but when his child is
born discovers overnight that strength is not enough,
and that he must learn gentleness.

— PAM BROWN

It's not unusual for the new father to spread the word about his newborn to anyone who will stand still long enough for pictures to be flipped out of his wallet. Most of the fathers we talked with waited until after the birth to collect snapshots. One father, however, was so excited about the arrival of his daughter, he paraded around with her picture from the sonogram!

Michael said, "The first time I saw her on the sonogram, I cried. I was so moved by seeing her heart beat. I thought she was so beautiful. Even though at first the picture is hard to make out, once I learned how to read the image I could see her nose was kind of lifted up in profile.

"I got a copy of the picture and carried it with me like most fathers do, only my kid wasn't born yet. I was waiting tables at the time, and I'd show all my customers a picture of my daughter. Most people just didn't get it. They'd say, 'What is that?' I'd show them and say, 'This is her head.' Some people would laugh and think I was crazy. The guys didn't appreciate it that much, but most of the women thought I was cute. Especially if they had kids of their own, they knew exactly what I was going through."

While it may be love at first sight for most fathers, the lasting bond that develops between daddy and daughter usually takes time, shared experiences, and a few dirty diapers! David told us that one of his first "bonding" experiences developed around the fact that his newly born daughter initially had trouble breast-feeding. Consequently, the baby lost weight at first. "To get her body weight back up," he told us, "every two hours Sophia would nurse her, and pump in-between to give her what she needed. I would get up every two hours to be with them. We did this for two weeks.

"One of the signs that all of this is working is a bowel movement, and she hadn't had one. There wasn't enough food going into her. She peed but she didn't have a movement. I deal with my anxiety with humor or song. Toward the end of that two-week period I was jostling her and came up with the song we now call the 'poo poo song':

> *My little baby's going to have a dirty diaper today*
> *We're going to dance on the ceiling.*
> *Mom, our little baby's going to have a dirty diaper today.*
> *We're going to dance all around*
> *Show it to the neighbors*

51

Gonna put it in their face,
Get a good smell, don't let 'em taste.
Call the grandparents, get 'em feeling proud
Tell the good news while I sing it loud.

"Believe it or not, she had a bowel movement that night. I think that would be called humorous musical prophecy."

David deepened the bond with his daughter by taking long walks with her. "We got an over-the-shoulder baby-holder, and from the time she was two weeks old I would take her for hour-long walks. It made me nervous at first, because I had thought that she would be sitting face out. Instead, she would nestle down, burrow down into the sling so that her head was against the bottom and her nose was mashed against the cloth. I thought, I'm surely going to kill my daughter! I'm going to come back from a walk and she's going to be dead. But I think she was putting herself back in the position she'd been in for the past month or so, which was really familiar and comfortable. I'd walk two miles from our home to Starbucks, have coffee, pat her, walk back. It was beautiful."

Not every father's experience of the first weeks of his daughter's life can be described as "beautiful." Michael's daughter had colic, and as any parent in that situation knows, babies can cry incessantly while parents try, often futilely, to find a way to comfort and quiet them. Michael recalled, "One of the very few things that she loved that made her stop crying for just a little bit was putting her in a swing. Other than that, most of the time it was horrible. There is nothing you can do. We tried all the remedies, but she cried all the time. Even my wife started crying, she was so frustrated. I mean, thank the Lord we didn't abuse our child. For three months, the crying seemed nonstop.

"Then the colic cleared up, and she stopped crying. I stood there and thought, 'Hey, she's actually fun. I used to love watching her make different kinds of faces. She was daddy's girl from the beginning, or at least from when she quit crying all the time!"

Michael told us how this bonding further deepened once his wife returned to part-time work and he spent a great deal of time caring for his newborn: "When my wife started working at night, I took care of her. That was an awesome thing for me and my daughter. It helped define our relationship from the beginning. I don't think a lot of fathers have the opportunity to spend the kind of time together we did."

Michael discovered something, as many fathers have, that a strong daddy-daughter bond takes time and energy to forge. The arrival may start with amazing excitement, but it's the day-in, day-out experiences that reflect what is truly possible in the bonding process.

Dreams I Had for My Little Girl

To show a child what has once delighted you, to find the child's delight added to your own so that there is now a double delight seen in the glow of trust and affection, this is happiness.

— J. B. PRIESTLEY

Most fathers have hopes and dreams for their children, especially for the daughters they adore. In many religious traditions, families gather for a ceremony welcoming the new infant into the community, a moment when fathers look ahead toward the baby's future.

Gary and his wife brought their daughter to church for a dedication ceremony when she was a few months old. Their church was not typical; services were held not in a traditional church sanctuary, but in a rented theater. He said, "We were meeting at Tennessee Performing Arts Center, which is an unusual place for a church to meet. We were asked to bring our daughter to the front for the dedication.

"It was so special to me, having her dedicated in that building, because it represented a combination of two very important aspects of my life: my faith and my career. I've never been one to follow the pack. I followed my dream and now work in the entertainment industry. I sing for a living. I stood there as my daughter was dedicated and thought about all the people who had played in that theater, and the different concerts, plays, and activities that had gone on within those walls. It seemed fitting to dedicate her there, as it represented the fulfillment of my artistic dreams joining together with my family. I hope and pray that my daughter will be able to fulfill her dreams as well."

Roy, another father known for his creative talent as an editor and publisher, also dreamed his daughters would achieve their artistic potential. "Even though my wife, Chris, and I divorced soon after our second daughter was born, we agreed on three goals for raising our daughters," he told us. "The first dream was to provide an atmosphere where the artistic and creative sides of who they are would be nurtured and supported. I didn't have that in my childhood, and I wanted something different for my girls.

"So, we did all kinds of play therapy and play learning experiences. Chris was especially good at this. The girls always had paints, clay, and paper — any art supply they wanted. Plus, we both filled our households with music, and of course, lots of books. I bought books for my daughters before they were even born!

"The second dream, related to the first, was the desire to expose them to the world of ideas, of culture. From the time they were two, I took them to see *The Nutcracker* every year. We took them to museums, cultural events, and art shows. I wanted my girls to feel comfortable with talking about ideas and feelings. Chris and I worked at this together, even after the divorce. If there was an event that wasn't technically my night, Chris would switch nights with me. As parents, we both promoted creativity and culture in our homes.

"The third dream was to create an environment where my girls were encouraged to take risks. Fathers usually do this for their sons, but not their daughters. Dads are often protective, if not overly protective, of their daughters. I wanted these girls to grow into women who felt they could do anything they wanted and were not afraid to try anything.

"For example, I remember taking the girls to the park when Erica was around four. She wanted to walk up the ladder and slide down by herself. I stayed close, in case she needed protection. But I didn't want to thwart her risk-taking efforts." Roy is seeing his dreams come true in the lives of his daughters, as they are both in college, expanding their education and their experiences of the world.

Some dreams that daddies have are focused on a particular event. Most of the time we imagine a mother being more interested than a father in dreams about a girl's wedding. In David's case, however, he's harboring a special hope for his daughter's someday wedding: "When my daughter was four months old, we went to Tunisia to attend a wedding. The place is stunningly beautiful, and a great place to visit, except for two weeks in August when it is blistering hot, and that's when we went.

"The wedding was a three-day affair. Three different

nights, three different styles and populations. I suppose because of the heat, festivities started at ten o'clock at night and went until two or three in the morning.

"After the wedding, we drove into the inner part of the country, where it's even hotter, to shop for carpets. While we were parking the car, a wind storm came up with rain, creating fast-driving pellets of sand. We couldn't get out of the car with Alexandra, but if we couldn't get out of the car, we couldn't buy carpets. So, I ran in and grabbed a small carpet to wrap her in to carry her into the shop. As it turned out, the carpet I grabbed was a tribal wedding shawl. So, we bought it. I hope that when she marries she'll use it some way in the ceremony."

Dreams come in all forms for a dad. The dreams a dad can have for his daughter may range from simple hopes of health and happiness to a devotion to cultivating the creative essence of his daughter. Dreams are more than just idle thoughts or powerless wishes, for as a father dreams, so will he teach, encourage, nurture, and guide. The hopes and dreams a woman has for herself are often shaped by those her father has for her. He can either close windows of opportunity, or open a world of possibilities for his little girl. That's why dreams are important for daddies and their daughters. Dreams keep us in tune with the present while adding hope for the future.

Section Two

Daddy's Girl

*I was my father's daughter. He is dead now and I am
a grown woman and still I am my father's daughter.
I am many things besides, but I am Daddy's girl,
too, and so I will remain — all the way to the old
folks' home.*

— PAULA WEIDEGER

*Every time I talk to my daughter, Linda Marie, I
say, "Linda Marie!" She yells back, "Daaaddy!!"
She also calls me "Daddylama" from when she first
heard about the Dalai Lama, 'cus she thinks I am so
wise! I still have her fooled at sixteen!*

— ALLEN, LINDA MARIE'S FATHER

I Knew She'd Be a Handful When . . .

*The "whys" hit two weeks ago. Before that, there were no whys.
Now there's a whole chain of whys, many whys. Why? We
answer, but, but but. She says, Why? We answer, but, but, but.
Sometimes she only stops when we get to God. We move into
metaphysics and then she's content. I use my ace:
"Because God loves you."*

— DAVID, ALEXANDRA'S FATHER

*My daughter's about a half bubble off dead center. I've lived
through the Smurf-blue hair, the blonde hair, the black hair,
and the green hair. I've lived through the nose rings
and the tongue rings. I've lived through it all.
You can deal with it as a problem, or see it as the gift it is.*

— JOHN, MELISSA'S FATHER

The blissful haze in a new father's eyes can be replaced
quickly with a stare of terror as he realizes his little girl
is made up of a few more things than sugar and spice
and everything nice. David got his first glimpse at what
he was up against when his daughter was only twenty-
three months old, and still breast-feeding. He told us, "I
was giving her a bath and suddenly she sits up in the
bath and says, 'Daddy, nay-nay.' She says 'Mommy, nay-
nay' when she wants to nurse. I said, 'You know I don't
have nay-nays.' She leans back and tilts her head and
says, 'Joke!'

"I knew I was in trouble. I thought, 'This child is not

two years old and she's already joking with me intelligently.' She knew that her mother had breasts (nay-nays), nipples, and milk. She knew that her grandmother had nay-nays, nipples, and no milk, and she knew that daddy had nipples but no nay-nays and no milk. I have this picture of her when she's sixteen running around laughing at me and I'm standing there going, 'What? What?' I already see my confusion."

If dads, like David, open their eyes early on, they will see clues about the personal strength and tenacity within their daughters. Lynn laughs about the time when her dad, Jeff, was trying to watch television on their new color set. Her mom, Mary Lynn, was washing dishes in the kitchen. Lynn reported, "Apparently, I had just figured out my strategy for life at five years old.

"The den and kitchen were all one big room, and I walked into the front area right by the television so I could get my daddy's attention. I said, proudly and with great conviction, 'Joe and Billy [my brothers] will always be five and seven years older than me. They will always be bigger, so I just have to be smarter!' I then tromped back to my room, the world now at peace, to play dolls."

Some fathers realize they have their hands full when they see how much their daughters take after themselves. Michael told us his daughter is very much like he was at her age: "She's very much of a people person. She'll talk to people on the street, just yell out to them, 'Hi! What's your name?' I was very talkative when I was little, too. I just went up to everybody and jabbered, although no one ever knew what I was saying most of the time." This social ability and ease with people can have its down side when fathers fear for their daughters' safety.

Pat worries about his daughter, who has taken on some of his personality traits. He said, "I am a little bit of a flirt, and my daughter is unequivocally a flirt. This is very scary for me, because she is a girl and could attract more attention than she can handle." Ah, yes, the apple often falls close to the tree.

Perhaps the surprised reaction we discovered among fathers we interviewed starts with the assumption that daughters will be more like their mothers than their fathers. There are many exceptions to that, to be sure. Dads know that if their little girls grow up with the same strengths and weaknesses they have, their daughters will have big dreams to pursue and, perhaps because of persistent sexual biases, these dreams will be somewhat harder to fulfill.

For example, Foster, father of five-year-old Hanna, loves to restore old cars. Foster reported, "Hanna seems to take quite a fancy to old cars, and is getting good at recognizing different kinds of cars. We really had a surprise last week when we were sitting outside of a restaurant, having a good time, eating dinner with some friends. Suddenly Hanna said, 'Daddy, Daddy, look across the road. Look over there. Parked in the parking lot, there's a 'Cuda.' All the people around us got a kick out of it. She pointed out a Plymouth Barracuda, and it dawned on me, this is something she picked up on her own. It made me come to a realization that your children want to honor you. They want to mimic you because you're their focal point for all of their cognitive learning."

Daughters do watch their fathers and try to emulate them. Brett, a commercial pilot, is a father who is proud of the fact that his daughter is a handful. When we interviewed him, he held a picture of his daughter lovingly in his hand. He said, "Recently, I came home from an overseas flight, dead tired. My little three-year-old, Kristen, comes running up with arms out, you know, 'Daddy's home!' I gave her a big hug. It's the sweetest way for coming home. It's just incredible.

"I looked over to where she was playing, and she had taken my flight jacket and my hat and put them on while she'd been on her riding horse. She called it her miniature airplane, and she was pretending she was a pilot. So there she was, just flying away.

"I don't know what she will ultimately want to do with her life. She might want to be more like her mother and go into the medical field. But for that moment, she was flying a plane, just like her daddy."

Knowing that their daughters may follow in their footsteps can sober even the most confident of dads. Tony, a big six-foot-five-inch man who envisions himself as a good basketball player, was talking about the top ten hardest things he'd ever done. He listed other basketball players who had outmaneuvered him or run faster, yelling humiliating things when he couldn't catch them. Finally, when he got to the number one hardest thing in his life, he said, "It was changing my daughter's diaper for the first time. I couldn't believe all that poop came out of that tiny little six-pound girl. I just didn't know what to do or where to start. Little did I know that was just the beginning of not knowing what to do to keep up with her. She doesn't know that I feel that way, but I sure do . . . daily."

What could be a bigger handful than a rambunctious daughter? Two rambunctious daughters — just ask Mark. He told us he knew he was in for a wild ride on the day of his father's funeral. His one-year-old daughter, Lyndsay, "unknown to us, toddled out onto the front porch and threw our car keys deep into the bushes. The confusion mounted throughout the morning, since we were scheduled to be at my father's house to ride in the hearse to his funeral. We missed our ride and caught a taxi to the church. Three days later, our yard man found them. We knew who the culprit was then!"

Mark Brooks's second daughter, Hallie, was not to be outdone by her older sister. As a pro golfer, Mark regularly takes the whole family with him as he tours. He told us, "After one of our trips, Hallie began to show signs of hearing loss, so we decided to take her to the doctor for a hearing test. While the doctor examined her ear, he said, 'Looks like an American Airlines peanut to me!' We still have the peanut that was buried deep in her ear. We put it in her scrapbook with the story."

It doesn't matter the size, intelligence, financial ability, or good looks of the man. Within her sphere of influence, a daughter has power over her dad far beyond even her own realization. She may be twenty-three months old or twenty-three years old, but when she decides to use that influence, it can be the sweetest, purest of blessings or the scariest of risks. Most of the time, dads pretend to be in charge, secretly knowing they're merely holding on for the ride of their lives.

The Value of Values

The child you want to raise as an upright and honorable person requires a lot more of your time than your money.

— GEORGE VARKY

Fathers told us, time and time again, how having a daughter brought out their protective, responsible sides. Perhaps self-focused or irresponsible in the past, dads were motivated to set a good example for their daughters, and to help them become women of strong character.

Michael told us how he used the opportunity of Christmas to teach his daughter the value of giving to others. "We're trying to be really careful raising her so that she doesn't take things for granted. We want her to know what Christmas is really about. One of the things we did this past year was to go to a housing project in town. We brought her along to show her that there are a lot of kids who don't have what she has and that she needs to be thankful for the quality of her life. I want to instill in her that giving is much better than receiving. So, she helped give presents out to these children, kids who have nothing compared to her.

"In the middle of the experience, one of the boys hit her and stole her balloon. She started crying. I sat down with her and told her that this boy didn't have a father, and because of that he may feel angry. She sat listening with wide eyes, and decided that she could forgive him.

In fact, that night she prayed for that little boy. She's becoming an example to me."

Fathers who have strong values related to politics, religion, or social issues can shape their daughters' values, but never control them. Dads who are too overbearing plant the seeds of rebellion they just might not enjoy once their little girls become teenagers. Dale, father of Nya, realized this truth when he told us, "I don't believe you can force your religious beliefs on children, but you can lead them in the right direction. When they're older, hopefully they'll make good decisions. We, as adults, don't make the best decisions all the time either. Freedom isn't worth having unless it includes the freedom to err. That's the philosophy that I have."

Many parents look around at society today with worried expressions, as the age of innocence seems to be shrinking. Many fathers want to protect their young daughters from the violence and explicit sexual material readily available to today's children. Dale echoed this concern; "You can look at the TV and the things that are out there. I think children in this day and age are exposed to more things than the people before this generation. I feel fortunate for the childhood I had. My parents instilled values and helped me see the difference between right and wrong. They empowered me to be responsible. I at least owe that to my daughter. I figure the more time I spend with her, the better. I know that I've invested in someone who can go out and be productive. With good values, she can be anything she wants to be."

The presence of a daughter can bring the best out in a man who wants to protect his little girl from the harsher aspects of life. Some fathers told us that having a daughter helped them live more consistently with their values, letting themselves off the hook less often. Bobby told us, "Although I have always had a clean vocabulary, as you would say, I would use four-letter words occasionally, as adjectives. But since I've had my daughter, there's no doubt that I've become much more aware of my vocabulary. I know she will repeat what she learns from me, and I don't want her to use profanity.

"That's not the only way I've cleaned up my act. She's given me a whole new perspective and sense of meaning in life. I've been around and I've had a variety of experiences. But when I had my daughter, I suddenly realized I was responsible for raising her and influencing how she was going to develop. How a father deals with his daughter early in life is going to be a very strong indicator of her later success in life. That becomes an incredible responsibility, and a real sense of purpose."

Many fathers today have very demanding schedules and don't have the quantity of time they desire with their daughters. Gary talked about how he and his wife deal with this problem: "We spend more time with our kids than most parents I know. We are blessed in that we own our own business, and I don't have to be at work at a certain time. I wake my daughter at sunup in the mornings. When I touch my sleeping daughter, she sits up and crawls into my arms without even opening her eyes. She knows her daddy is there. We sit there on her bed and hug for a few precious moments every morning. I then fix my children breakfast, pack their lunches, get them dressed, and take them to school. After that, I go to work.

"A lot of people don't understand why I don't like to travel as much as I used to. It won't be too long before the opportunity to hug my daughter on her bedside in the mornings is gone. Kids grow up fast. So I want to enjoy this time as much as I can. My kids are my priority.

"I think back on some of the significant events in my life that have influenced how I am as a parent, and I think about a relationship which began when I was about sixteen. I went to see a friend, JoAnne, who had been sick, and I took her a two-cent Tootsie Roll pop. The next time I saw her, she told me what a very special person I was. Prior to that, I had never thought about it, but what she said had a permanent impact on me. From then on, I wanted to be that 'special' person she thought I was.

"As our friendship developed, I spent a lot of time at JoAnne's house. I quickly realized that JoAnne and her father, Stan, had a very special relationship. JoAnne could talk to her dad about anything you can imagine, and did. He instilled in her, and in his other children, a solid understanding that they were special, and that they could achieve anything they wanted if they applied themselves. Stan also taught his children to recognize the specialness in other people and to communicate that to those people. I am convinced that one of the reasons why I have gotten to where I am today is that I wanted to live up to JoAnne's expectations of me.

"I coveted that relationship she had with her father. Even though I was just a teenager, I made a personal commitment to try to have that same kind of relationship if I ever had a daughter. Now I do have a daughter. My mission is to be a special dad and to instill in Jordyn an understanding that she is special and can accomplish anything she wants to do. We talk about everything. There is nothing off-limits. I cherish these talks, and I look forward to the more challenging subjects that will come as she grows. The same goes for my son."

Some fathers generate opportunities for a young girl's character to grow. Michael told us a story about how he helped teach his daughter the importance of sharing. He said, "One of Megan's favorite things is drinking a glass of milk that has a cherry at the bottom. She was drinking her milk and she could not wait to get to the bottom to eat that cherry. And I waited and I waited and at the last minute, she was almost to the cherry, and I asked her, 'Can Daddy have your cherry?' I know this sounds cruel, but I was going to teach her a lesson.

"She looked at me, and she said, 'Yeah, you can have my cherry.' So I ate the cherry. She just went on eating her dinner like there was nothing to it. I went to the refrigerator and got her two cherries. I brought them back, and I said, 'Here.' And she said, 'Oh, I just wanted one.' She ended up giving the other one to her brother.

Her mommy and I really try to teach her to be giving and to not complain. And she did that yesterday, and it just melted my heart."

It can be difficult at times, however, to know who is the teacher and who is the student, the dad or the daughter. David told us about how Alexandra, who is nearly three, taught him and his wife a lesson in dealing with conflict: "Sometimes she will see things in a different way. It helps for me to see things from her eyes. When she was maybe two years old, Sophia and I were starting to argue. Alexandra grabbed my face and pulled it to look at her. Staring deep into my eyes, she said, 'That is *not* a good idea!'

"I looked back at her and said, 'You're right. That's not a very good idea.' So we stopped. I believe in her perception. The arguing was not a good idea. We used to pay a counselor a lot of money for that kind of advice!"

Values come in all sorts of packages, whether you get your advice from a therapist, a daddy, or a daughter. One doesn't know how or when these lessons will show up in life. The challenge is to embrace what is before us and learn from it.

Accidents and Illnesses

I can't imagine anything worse than losing a child.
— DAVID, ALEXANDRA'S FATHER

Dads have a tough job. On one hand, they long to protect their little girls from any hurt or pain. On the other, children often look to their fathers for a sense of self-confidence. Knowing that your dad believes in you is all some of us have needed to take the risks necessary to succeed in life. Balancing risk-taking with a "be careful, don't get hurt" attitude can be a challenge for dads who want their daughters to be both safe and competent.

David, father of three-year-old Alexandra, felt the crunch of these two concerns when he first began to teach Alexandra how to swim. He told us, "Now she loves to swim, and I'm thrilled she is so comfortable in the water. Before she learned to swim, I tried to get her to sit in a floaty device we have in the pool here. She sat on the steps in the shallow end and wasn't particularly interested in my idea. In my effort to entice her to sit in this thing, I played with it, swimming back and forth from the shallow end to the deep end, showing her how much fun it was.

"When I was at the other end of the pool, she lost her balance. I watched her fall down into the water with a surprised look on her face. She couldn't understand what was happening. I swam back so fast and lifted her out and she said, 'Boomah'—that's what she says when she falls down. It wasn't a defining experience for her at all. But for me, the thought of losing her is the worst thing I can imagine."

Swimming pools seem to be places where many childhood dramas take place, as more than one father told us about accidents around the water. George described a time when his little girl, Alison, went on an unexpected swim at the age of one and a half: "She was riding her tricycle out by the pool, and somehow managed to back it up into the pool. She hadn't learned to swim yet and just sunk to the bottom. Both my wife, Melanie, and I raced over and pulled her out, but she wasn't breathing.

"We went through the CPR routine, and she coughed a bunch of water out. We were pretty scared at that point. So I told Melanie, 'Don't worry, she's okay.' I wasn't sure I believed it, but I didn't need her mom hyperventilating at that point. We took her down to the hospital and everything turned out okay. I don't think, however, I have ever been that scared in my life."

Dave is another father who knows what it's like to feel scared for his little girl's safety. In fact, the scare of his life came on Father's Day, not too long ago. He told us, "My wife, Carla, my three children, and I had a great Father's Day morning together, doing all the fun things we do on such days: sleeping in, homemade cards, and special treatment. I loved it.

"That evening, our church fellowship group met at a neighborhood park for a picnic. My wife wasn't feeling well, so I took my two sons and Ellie, my daughter, with me. I was a little apprehensive taking Ellie because she had recently been diagnosed with a rare blood condition called ITP, short for idiopathic thrombocytopenia, that causes the white blood cells to destroy the platelets. No platelets, no clotting of the blood.

"ITP first made itself known to us by bruises on Ellie's legs. At first we thought, 'That's nothing to worry about. Any six-year-old gets plenty of them, especially Ellie.' Her favorite thing to do at school was play on the monkey bars. She was a natural climber. Not good for her mother's nerves, but she was careful and rarely fell. Then we noticed that the bruises were unusually dark in color. When she got a bee sting and showed signs of bruising, we took her straight to the doctor.

"When the doctor told us, 'She has ITP,' I felt the combination of a sudden chill and being hit in the stomach. I knew what ITP was. The son of good friends of ours had been fighting for his life for several months from this rare blood condition. I knew it was potentially fatal. They sent us to specialists in the area and we had an appointment the very next day, a Friday, I recall.

"The staff at the center was great, conveying a calm professionalism that was a great comfort for two scared parents. Ellie had an IV treatment, and we were told to come back to see if she would respond to the medication. It was a long weekend.

"Finally Monday arrived. Unlike our friends' son, Ellie responded well to the medication and her platelet levels rose significantly. She was still in danger, but we were hopeful. We knew that until her levels rose higher, she was at risk of stroke. Bleeding in the brain was a very serious possibility, because her blood didn't clot properly. The doctor told us it could take years before her platelet levels returned to normal. There was nothing we could do except keep a close watch on her and return to the doctor for weekly blood tests.

"With that fresh in my mind, I kept a close eye on Ellie as she played with the other children at the park. Sitting with the other parents, I became engaged in a lively discussion when I heard Ellie's cry. I looked up and she was wobbling toward me with her hand over her forehead. Blood was pouring out of the wound. I grabbed a towel and called for a friend to drive me home. Another friend volunteered to care for my two sons while we rushed Ellie away.

"As soon as we got home, my wife jumped in the van and we sped off to the hospital. I looked down at the lovely child in my arms. I knew that there are no guarantees in life. Many parents have been through more than I, but this was still life-threatening. I prayed silently, begging God to help, knowing that I have no right to a pain-free life. Not knowing how to pray, I said, 'Lord, help us.' I looked down at the wound and the bleeding had almost stopped. The pressure bandage was working.

"Ellie was a trouper. She handled the exam with a lot of poise for a child her age. They called in a plastic surgeon, because the gash was visible, across her forehead and into her eyebrow. The surgery went off without a hitch. She looked sad, but cute in a funny way, with the bandage on her head. She liked the bandage, in fact. I think she was a little proud of it, and of herself and how she handled the surgery.

"The doctor told us, 'Thankfully her platelet levels seem good since her blood clotted so well. But you must be careful. She may have a concussion from the fall, and we must be sure she doesn't have a brain hemorrhage.'

"We were so emotionally exhausted, sleep was what we needed. However, sleep was something we wouldn't get for quite a while. We put Ellie between us in bed and set the alarm to go off every hour. All night long, hour after hour, we checked her. After ten hours of watching her, seeing that she was fine, we finally got to sleep.

"The next day she was back to her old self. In fact, from that point, her platelet count has made a steady climb up to normal. Her symptoms haven't returned, and as for the scar on her eyebrow? The surgeon turned out to be one of the highest rated plastic surgeons in the area. The scar is hardly visible, even when you look right at it. I don't know why these things happen. But I do believe God uses these times to strengthen us. We've certainly grown stronger as a family, and more grateful of each day we have together. I've become very protective of my little girl."

That protective spirit comes alive when Daddy's little girl is in danger. Carmen recalled a time when her father came to her rescue, risking his own life to save hers. She said, "I was around ten years old and we went to stay in a mountain cabin for the first time. I'd had no experience climbing, but took to the cliffs behind the cabin as soon as we got unpacked. I met a couple of other kids my age who knew how to move up and down the slopes quickly. As we headed back down, I lost my balance and slid, flipped, and flopped for a total of one hundred and fifty feet! My father, who was chopping wood on the side of the slope, saw me falling and threw himself after me, trying to stop my fall. I can still remember my mom screaming from down below as she watched us both tumble down the mountainside. I flew into the air, over boulders the size of small houses, and landed on the only patch of sand around.

"My parents scurried to my side and we all hobbled back to the cabin. I was scratched up from head to foot, but escaped without any broken bones. My dad had a huge gash, and I remember feeling so grateful that he loved me so much he'd be willing to risk his own safety for me. Needless to say, the vacation was over and we drove back home and to the doctor's office that same night. But as far as I was concerned, my dad was my hero."

Dads running to the rescue was a theme we discovered in our interviews. Bradley is another dad who ran to help his daughter, Tricia, when he and his wife saw her pass out on the football field while marching in the school band. He recalled, "I could see her marching around the perimeter of the track. They were coming off the field, coming back to their seats. They were probably one hundred yards away, when she just collapsed. She had suffered from asthma all her life, and we knew immediately what the problem was.

"I jumped over the railing and ran down the track. My wife couldn't get over the fence because she was wearing a skirt. But I sprinted across the track. I was gone. By the time that I got there, some of her friends had helped her sit up. Then we took her to the hospital and spent several hours there for treatment. She scared us half to death."

Dads can come through for their daughters in many ways when they're sick or hurt. Lynn recalled a time when her dad made all the difference for his sick little girl. She said, "I remember I had a very high temperature. Since I was a very extroverted, precocious child, it was extremely hard to lie there in bed. All my relatives were visiting, but I was stuck in my room. I hated being alone, so I weakly called out for everything I could, just to have someone come into my room so we could talk. Normally I was the center of attention . . . and I wasn't even in the den where everyone was gathered. I couldn't believe my mother actually expected me to rest with all that activity happening without me!

"Finally, against my mom's wishes, my daddy came in and picked me up out of bed and took me into the den. He laid me on the couch so I could rest my head in his lap. That very act calmed my distress. I remember as I went off to sleep, my dad saying, 'Her forehead is so hot you could fry an egg on it!' Everyone laughed, I smiled, and now, I could relax, since I was, for a minute, the center of attention once again."

Daughters aren't the only ones who get sick or have accidents. Sometimes, dads get into trouble and it's the daughters who want to make it okay. George told us about how his three-year-old daughter reacted when he had a heart attack. He recalled, "I had the heart attack a few days before her fourth birthday, and had to spend a week in the hospital. At school, while I was still in the hospital, the kids started to sing *Happy Birthday* to her and she made them stop. She told everybody at her kindergarten that she was 'postponing' her birthday until her daddy came home! That was pretty nice. When I was in intensive care, my wife was the only one who could see me, so my daughter had to wait. When I finally came home, we had her birthday party. All of our friends came over and celebrated, a full week after her party was originally scheduled. Imagine a child being willing to wait for her own birthday so her daddy could be there! I suppose that if I hadn't come home, she'd have been three forever!"

Little girls and big girls alike worry about their fathers' health. Linda, a flight attendant based out of Chicago, told us about her concern when her father recently had surgery: "I knew he was really worried about the surgery, so my sister and I talked about what we should do. I called my dad the night before the surgery, but I didn't tell him we were coming in to see him. He acted like that was fine, but I could tell he was nervous. He asked, 'You're going to call me when this is all over, aren't you?' and I said 'Oh Dad, don't worry, I'll be there.' And as soon as he came out of surgery, we were there with a big stuffed teddy bear and balloons. When he saw us he started crying. It was so cool!"

Dads and daughters need each other when they are sick or hurt. We daughters need our dads to run to hold us and make sure we get the help we need. They need us to encourage them and let them know no one in this world can replace them. Both would like to go through life unscathed from the mishaps, catastrophes, and traumas life holds. But that is not to be, and within the daddy-daughter relationship there is a place of consolation from the disturbances that come on a moment's notice.

School Days

Fathers know their baby girls are growing up when they reach school age. That first day can be traumatic, for child and parents alike. This can be especially challenging as today's children go to child care and preschool at an earlier age than in the past. Michael told us about his daughter's first day in preschool, which was about a month and a half before we spoke with him. He said, "My wife cried, so I brought [my daughter] into the classroom. She looked at me and crawled up onto my lap, hugging me, and she wouldn't let me go. So I said, 'Hey look! Here's your chair. It's got your name on it.'

"She got a little excited and smiled. Then she saw a friend of hers and everything was okay. She was so cute. She was excited yet she was nervous to be left alone. Once I left, she was fine. I left thinking, 'My little girl is not so little anymore.' I tried not to feel depressed, because there is joy in her getting older. Yet it's hard to let go of her, knowing that she'll be up against kids that

82

aren't so nice and I won't be there to protect her. That's the hardest part. Not being able to protect her as much as when she was younger and always at home."

Michael's not alone in this sentiment. Vito also struggled when his daughter first attended school. "First two or three months of school she cried every single day," he lamented. "It was awful. She would tell me, 'Dad, you don't understand how much I love you.' I would say, 'Ange, you gotta go to school, you gotta.' I finally went home and told my wife 'The next time she does that, I'm taking her right home. I just can't take it, she kills me!' Fortunately for dad and daughter, Ange has settled into school now. But the temptation to rescue their daughters from harm, or even emotional distress, can be a powerful force for most dads.

The urge to protect one's daughter is not limited to fathers of preschoolers or kindergarten students. John found himself feeling mighty protective of his sixth-grade daughter, Melissa: "I was at a parent-teacher meeting, and her teacher was saying that Melissa doesn't conform, and he intended to make her conform. I said, 'No you are not! You have to understand, Melissa has a gift of seeing things differently than everybody else does.'

"Melissa sees things from an angle, from a different perspective. And she has the ability to describe in words what she is seeing. I told the teacher that this talent was not a problem to be solved, that it was a gift from God for the rest of the world. My responsibility as a father and parent is to nurture that, and to protect her when I can from people who want to squelch that special quality in her.

"I have to teach her to stay within the white lines, so she doesn't get into too much trouble. I can't let her run off the edge of the road. There are rules for life. But I also don't want to hurt or dampen her ability to see things differently, and to be able to describe what she sees.

"So the teacher and I had to come to an understanding. He was an ex-police officer who wanted everyone to be the same. He wanted them to sit in the same position, with their feet the same. His concept of discipline was uniformity. But that's not discipline, that's over-control."

John was not the only father called to school because his daughter needed a little extra encouragement to behave. Toby received a phone call to come to school immediately to help out with a problem his six-year-old daughter was creating. Toby laughed when he told us about how his daughter, Lori, had become very attached to the school bus driver: "The bus driver was quitting and Lori didn't want him to leave. So, she laid down under the tires of the school bus and the school bus could not move forward or backward. They had to call me to come get her out from under the school bus. I went and pulled her out by her feet because they wouldn't touch her. Then I explained to her that the bus driver needed to quit for his own reasons and she would have to accept this. Eventually she did, but boy, did she ever make her feelings known!"

Discipline around schoolwork can be especially challenging for those who have chosen to home-school their children, as more and more parents are doing these days. Alex told us, "My wife home-teaches all of our kids, so we don't have to deal with disagreements with school personnel. I recently had a challenge with my daughter, however, when my wife left for a meeting and I was left to teach the kids for a couple of hours. They brought their schoolwork into the family room and we were working together. My youngest, Whitney, who's eight, had to memorize Egyptian hieroglyphics, what the forms mean, and then how to write her name in that language. She had one page that she was supposed to memorize, and at first she annoyed her brother and sister by reading it out loud. I told her she'd have to go into another room if she wanted to read out loud. She stomped off, then returned and threw the paper on the floor saying she was done.

"I said, 'Give me that. Okay, how many hieroglyphic forms are there?'

"She said, 'I don't know.'

" 'What year did the French, whatever-his-name-was, figure out what the ruins meant?'

" 'I don't know.'

"So I said, 'Take it back. You didn't memorize it.' And she cried and cried. Of course, I felt like the bad taskmaster.

"She said, 'I'm only supposed to know it a little bit. Just read through it so I can pronounce the words.

That's really all I have to do, just, you know, so that I can say the big words on the page.'

"I laughed, and said, 'You know I love you but you're lying through your teeth. Take this page and go learn it.' She stomped off crying, but about twenty minutes later, she came back and said, 'Got it.' I asked her three questions, and she got 'em all right.

"I said, 'Now, how do you feel?' and she got this big smile on her face, and she said, 'I know it,' and I said, 'That's right.'

"When her mom came home, I said, 'Go 'head, test her on that Egyptian stuff and see.' Whitney got a big old smile on her face, full of confidence and she said, 'Go ahead,' and she handed my wife the paper. So it was a sense of accomplishment for her, a pride thing; it was good knowing inside herself she could do it."

Expecting daughters to achieve in school is a pressure many of us women remember well. Handing report cards to our dads to review, hoping for approval, is a memory many daughters recall with fear and trembling. Performing well academically is stressful, regardless of the grade one may be in, but it was all the more challenging for Sophia, a woman we spoke with who spent her girlhood days in Beirut. She told us, "Education was always very important to my father. He's the one who would come for parent-teacher meetings. Of course, related to that concern were the big black felt-marker circles around the Cs on my report card: 'Needs more homework.'

"I'd always done well in school. I was always the teacher's favorite, always the person with potential. But my father was a perfectionist, so as much as I got affirmation, I also had him pressuring me. He didn't seem to realize how much more difficult it was for me because I went to a school where classes were taught in French and Arabic. I was learning three languages while learning the subjects taught in the class. French wasn't just French, it was math, history, science, physics, geology. On top of that, I had the same subjects in Arabic, too. Everything in three languages. I remember him helping me with my math in English, even though I had to translate it back into French in the classroom. I had no one at home to help me with my homework in French and Arabic, so at times I felt like he was disappointed in me."

For fathers who care, pressure is often the flip side of support, disappointment the flip side of pride. Those fathers who want their daughters to succeed can be those who simultaneously offer a refuge of encouragement and the source of distress. The softer, more protective side of Sophia's father was demonstrated when, due to civil war in Beirut, the family had to flee and her family members were dispersed all over the world. Abruptly, Sophia was taken from her multilingual school and brought to the States to attend boarding school in Massachusetts.

Sophia's eyes welled up as she recalled, "One really poignant moment showed me how hard it was for him to leave me at boarding school. I'd only been there a week and he'd taken my brother to begin school in Saratoga

Springs, New York. He came back to visit me on his way to London. It was Sunday and he walked me to chapel. It was really cold and already snowing. We stood at the chapel door. He said, 'If you're not happy here, we'll find some place else for you to go. You don't have to stay.'

"At that moment I knew I had a choice. And I remember saying to him, 'No, I like it here. I want to stay.' I felt like this was a place I wanted to stay. I was being strong, but also honest. I knew in my heart that he wanted the best for me. There was always choice, especially when it was a lifetime-changing event. It wasn't, 'You've got to go there' or 'You have to stay here.'

"That moment when we said good-bye, I knew we weren't going to see each other for a long time. He hugged me and I thought I was going to die. He hugged me so tightly I could hardly breathe. It was so sad. And when he turned away from me, he was crying. I remember standing there watching him walk away, and I knew he was crying, and it was so hard because I really missed my dad. I still get emotional about it. That was the year my family fell apart. That was the last time I lived at home with my parents. My life would have been really different if my family had stayed together, and I've become a different person because of it. I'm grateful for the person I am today, but I became an adult at that moment. I had to make a lot of adult decisions. There was a lot of pressure on me, external and wanting to live up to my own ideals. Making my own plans. But I'd learned a lot from my dad by watching him. I felt like he trusted me with a lot of responsibility."

From the beginning of preschool to school days away from home, it's the time when daughters begin to learn how we fit into the world. Our fathers' expectations can help or hinder our movement from the home to finding a place among our peers. Our dads have the opportunity to watch how they influence, mold, and shape us, and to watch how this impact sets the stage for all we accomplish once we're grown.

$$$$$

Having a girl is God's way of saying:
"You'll never have enough money!"

— BOB, FATHER OF ASHLEY AND ALYSE

A father is a banker provided by nature.

— FRENCH PROVERB

It was the day before Valentine's Day and Lynn was in the sixth grade. The prize was ahead of her. It was a baking contest in Mrs. Tucker's class for the best Valentine's dessert. Lynn had decided on a red velvet heart-shaped cake. It's a difficult cake to get just right from scratch. She only had one heart-shaped pan and, true to form, she started the process a bit late for the complexity of the situation. The cake should be done by nine P.M., cooled by ten P.M., and icing on the cake — voilà! — in bed by ten-thirty P.M. to go for the gold the next day. That was the plan that would never come to fruition.

The dominoes starting falling around eight twenty-five P.M. The first layer of this two-layer cake came out of the oven flat. Do you know what a really thick one-inch red-colored chocolate pancake looks like? That's close. Big tears welled up in Lynn's eyes. Her dad was watching a television show in mindless relaxation. He heard the whimpering and got up and came into the kitchen from the den.

"What's the problem?" Almost before he could finish he *saw* the problem. He walked over, picked up the recipe, and started asking questions; after all, one half of the cake batter still remained. Lynn continued, "After he gently grilled me on all the ingredients, we determined I had forgotten the baking powder. The main problem now was that I couldn't half the recipe to make another layer, because we didn't have enough of the ingredients. So dad told me to add the baking powder appropriately and cook the next layer. In the meantime, at nine P.M. at night he would go out and buy more ingredients. This was in the 1960s and the problem was that all the grocery stores in our area were closed by nine in those days. I didn't realize that at the time, but dad did. Being competitive even as a child, I was just so happy that I now had a chance at the prize again. I got busy mixing and cooking.

"By nine forty-five P.M. the second, now beautiful, layer had come out of the oven," Lynn remembered. "I had the heart-shaped pan greased and floured and there was no daddy. I was beside myself." Time was slipping, slipping into the future. Finally, at 10:15 P.M. her dad walked into the house carrying a bag full of the needed supplies. "He had hit every grocery store from the east side of town and found one open all the way across town. On top of that, he had found these little clear red heart candies to decorate the cake adding more flare to my creation." Lynn got to bed around midnight that night, worn out.

"Dads attending school functions can be a highlight to

daughters," Lynn recalled, "The next day was the only day that I can remember that my dad came to my school in my educational life. Several mothers came, but my dad was the only guy there. He was dressed in a suit, he had probably attended a business meeting earlier that day. I was lucky he hadn't come in filthy from the oil field. Sure enough, when the winner for cakes was announced, it was me. Then there was a winner for candy, pies, and other kinds of dessert. Almost breathlessly, we all waited to see who would win the overall prize of the day. My dad kept smiling and encouraging me, while he ate a piece of my cake. Finally, they called all the winners up and my name was announced as winner of the All Around Best Valentine's Day Dessert.

"He didn't have to go out and spend that extra money or time for me. I don't know if he ever did anything like that for my brothers. But for me, it meant the world. At the time, he probably wondered why he was buying cake ingredients and little clear red candies past his bedtime, but for me it seemed like that's what a dad does when his little girl needs him."

Adopting a "nothing is too good for my daughter" attitude is common among the proud fathers we interviewed. Jeff, president of a record company and father of a daughter in preschool, told us, "I want my daughter to have the best of everything, especially in schooling. My wife and I decided we wanted her to go to private school. So, we started looking into private kindergarten. When I found out the prices, I immediately thought of a second job. Not only that, my daughter has to perform, try out, for the privilege of me paying six thousand dollars a year . . . and this is just kindergarten!" (He hasn't faced college yet.)

The process of being admitted to this private kindergarten program is tantamount to an audition. He continued, "You have to pay a $100 to $200 deposit for her to come to the school for a 'play day' for the teachers to observe her. The catch is that you have to do four or five of these deposits so you are guaranteed (in your mind) that she'll make it in. The preschool teacher fills out a questionnaire about your daughter, then observes while your child plays. Next, a teacher goes to her preschool and observes her in there. We went through all of this to make sure that our precious daughter is not denied anything! I stirred myself up internally, wondering, 'Is the thirty-five-hundred-dollar school really as good as the six-thousand-dollar school?' It's an amazing process and funny. You don't, won't really know if all this is worth it. I just call it 'education insurance.'"

Jeff also shared with us differences experienced in raising a girl versus raising a boy. "When I first got married I was stunned at the prices of lady's lingerie and how many different kinds and colors they feel they need. It's the same with little girls' clothes. One pair of tights costs nine dollars and with the first roll in the grass they're gone. I know for a fact we have three different shades of pink in her room right now." He continued about other little-girl accessories: "And hair bows, barrettes, and ties, oh my goodness! If I could sell back all the hair bows we've bought at half the price, I'm pretty sure I could finance a Third World country."

Then this dad told us about a woman's plague — shoes: "Shoes, ahhhh, every size, we have to get the tennis shoes, casual shoes, and the dress shoes (and any boots, flip-flops or the like, depending on the season). The amazing thing is, my wife says we can go to a department or discount store and I say, while bleeding on the inside, 'Oh no, let's go to Nordstrom.' I hate buying cheap clothes. Only quality clothes for *my* daughter." We asked him why. He replied, "Because she's my precious baby girl. I am also pretty positive that the shoes from a super discount store will deform her feet simply because they cost less. I know this is factually untrue, and probably not logical, but that's what I find myself doing almost every time. I will, however, buy good shoes on sale."

He added, "It does amaze me that I will buy good quality clothing, with a life expectancy of five years, when I know good and well that it's only going to be on her body for four to six months." These are the actions clearly of a daddy who realizes his devotion to his daughter is motivation to continue working hard in his career.

However, Jeff is not alone in his shopping woes. John, the single parent of four girls, told us this story about the challenge of tampons. He said, "Inevitably they all will run out of tampons when I'm the only one still dressed. I get, 'Pleeeeeeease, daddy, I have *got* to have them. I don't want to go out tonight. I feel horrible and it's dark.' Because the dread is so overwhelming, I always forget to bring up the fact that they don't have a problem going out to a movie when it's dark. I get my billfold, because this isn't cheap, slip into my penny loafers, grab a coat, and with shoulders drooping I am on my way to get this buying extravaganza over as soon as possible."

Then he described the emotional fun he goes through in the grocery store: "It's a lot better these days. Especially with women, they would look at me and smile like — poor guy. The guys just look at the boxes and we start talking football. The more boxes I have, the more details we talk about in the most recent Cowboys game. Obviously, I would try to find a *guy* at the checkout. The object of the game was to get out of there as fast as possible. You have to weigh whether to stand there longer with the boxes in plain view or go to the girl at the checkout who might loudly proclaim, 'I wish *my* husband would buy Tampax for me. Your wife must really think you're wonderful.' Then I have to mumble, 'No, it's for my daughters.' I hate the talkative checkout girls, because that elicits even more exclamations and attention, which I am trying to avoid at all cost.

"Now, it's more common to see other men in the aisle, along with me. The worst part is when all four girls want different kinds and you have to be on the aisle for more than twenty seconds. There are hundreds of brands, all in different-colored boxes, but with one slight difference on the box. There are different shapes, strengths, and even scented or unscented. I can't even believe I know all of that. It's information I never thought I would want to know. It's especially embarrassing if you have to help a new young guy who's lost on that aisle of feminine hygiene insanity. He looks at you thankfully for the help, but you know he's thinking, 'Oh man, what am I in for with this deal?'

"It's very easy to get back to the house and find I have botched the effort altogether. So, I can have spent well over twenty dollars and humiliated myself in one fell swoop, be wrong, with no thanks, and get in trouble for the effort. I am willing to go through this humiliation, though, because I know my girls have to have these things and I don't want them to suffer. That's what I tell myself anyway."

From tuition and school projects to pretty outfits and "young lady" needs, dads are called on to dig deep into their pockets and make it happen for their daughters. They may complain, but the fathers we talked to always had a smile on their faces, remembering the joy they brought to their daughters. After all, nothing, and we mean *nothing*, is too good for Daddy's little girl.

Summer Camps and
Leaving Dad Behind

She loved camp. That only made it rougher for me.

— PAT, EMILY'S FATHER

*You can get back into the car! I can carry my backpack
by myself, Dad.*

— ESTHER, WILLIAM'S DAUGHTER

Augh! the pain of separation that can occur when daddy's little girl grows up enough to actually go away to camp! While we daughters excitedly pack for our new adventure away from home, our dads can be sadly anticipating one of the first of many separations. Pat told us how hard it was for him to have his nine-year-old daughter leave for summer camp — not that this camp business was his idea, mind you. He said, "My wife wanted our daughter to have the experiences of camp like she did, so she made arrangements with a camp in New Hampshire. I didn't even dream how much I would miss her. After the first day, though, I was devastated!

"We weren't allowed to call the camp for the first two weeks. I had no idea what was going on — whether my daughter liked the camp, did not like it, was having a good time or bad. It was really frustrating for me. I couldn't do anything.

"After two weeks, I got a couple of letters. They made

me want to talk to her more to find out if she was *really* happy. I just wondered if they were brainwashing her or something. Then we got this letter where she told us she'd chipped her tooth while on a hike in the woods and the kids started making fun of her the next day. She was really upset about this. Now she hated camp and didn't like anybody.

"I hadn't seen my daughter for three weeks, so this letter got me all worked up. I was devastated all over again. I was ready to drive six hours to New Hampshire and bring her back. So, without my wife knowing, I called the camp and talked with a counselor. She told me that they were having dinner and she would check it out and call me back at ten-thirty P.M. I just sat by the telephone waiting for this counselor to call back about my daughter. I didn't leave the phone for four and a half hours!

"It turned out that everything was fine. My daughter had chipped her tooth, but everyone had dealt with it and moved on to other events, so I let it slide, because I knew we were going up the next week for parents' visiting day. All the parents visit on the same day. It was great to see her. She was so proud of her camp. We just had a great time.

"Then this amazing thing happened when we were leaving. You are saying good-bye to your kid, and suddenly one kid starts crying hysterically, and then another and another. There's a whole bunch of counselors holding them back because they want to leave with their parents. It's like leaving them in prison. Sarcastically I said to my wife, 'Yeah, This is a really good time, honey. I am glad we did this.' We left my daughter there, and then as we drove off, I just lost it. I was no different than those hysterical kids. I was just a hysterical father. I cried quite a while before I settled down."

While going off to camp can be traumatic, sometimes the experience can bring fathers and daughters closer together, as Jessica discovered when she went off to camp beginning in the fifth grade. She said, "My folks were divorced. Although both of my parents lived in the same town, I spent most of my time with my mom. From the age of ten on, I went to summer camp four years in a row. My first time was special, because Dad and I wrote letters to each other all the time. At the end of the two-week summer camp, there would be a rodeo. Every year my dad showed up for that rodeo. It set up a tradition for my dad and me to be in communication during camp. In fact, that's when I felt the closest to him, even though we lived fairly close to each other. I look back now on that, and it's something that I could count on, for him to be there at that rodeo watching me ride in the rodeo parade and barrel riding."

There are all kinds of summer camps. Many are just for recreation, others are for educational purposes that help the child get ahead in the school year. One such camp is a band camp. Lynn recalled the time when she went to West Texas State University band camp: "During one particular band camp, I think after the eighth grade, I decided I wanted to look more like a particular movie star. I believe it was Elizabeth Taylor. I dyed my hair pitch black from mousy brown. I have a very fair complexion, with deep blue eyes. I thought it looked quite dramatic.

"When I got home, my mother completely freaked out. At that stage, I would just stare at my parents whenever they did something I didn't like, and say, 'I don't know' to any question.

"It went like this:

" 'Why in God's name and all that's right in the world did you dye your hair black?'

" 'I don't know.'

" 'You look awful, like a cheap hussy. Don't you realize that?'

" 'I don't know.'

" 'You just wait 'til your dad gets home. You just wait! Do you want to know what he'll do?'

" 'I don't know. I don't care. I like it. There's nothing you can do. It's permanent.'

"So dad came home from a hard day out in the oil fields of West Texas. He was excited because he knew his little girl would be home after two weeks away. Things, in his view, had been way too quiet.

"My dad walked in the front door yelling, 'Is my baby home? Where is my girl?' Knowing I was in deep trouble with Momma, I ran to him, letting him know how desperately I missed him. I started telling him immediately of stories I knew he would like about band camp. He loved me to win at twirling . . . and I did.

"Mom could take it no more. She finally lost it and said, 'Can you believe her hair?' Dad, visually unobservant, said, 'Yes, yes . . . I love it!' Of course, he wasn't exactly sure what it was he liked. But he knew he didn't want trouble right at that moment. Unfortunately, that was not to be his lot in life that day.

"I yelled in victory at the top of my lungs. Mom just walked back to her bedroom seething. Dad, dazed, asked what he did wrong. I told him he was just perfect. I thought it was a good plan, but he still headed back to the bedroom. Ten minutes later I was in the shower washing the nonpermanent dye out of my hair to become his mousy-brown-headed little girl once again."

Separated from their daughters, perhaps for the first time since their daughters' birth, dads are often left at home wondering if their daughters will find that "absence makes the heart grow fonder" or "out of sight" he's now out of mind.

Going off to camp can change a daughter in more ways than one, sometimes helping her grow more independent of her father. But hopefully a little time away will help her value her dad all the more, once daddy's girl is back home.

Our Special Time Together

*Dads are stone skimmers, mud wallowers, water wallopers,
ceiling swoopers, shoulder gallopers upsy-downsy,
over-and-through, round-and-about whooshers. Dads are
smugglers and secret sharers.*

— HELEN THOMSON

*My dad and I went on a trip to Hawaii. After we checked in to
the hotel, we went swimming. It was great! We went to
California Pizza Kitchen the next night. The next day we
saw the dolphins. They were awesome! Then, at the end of
the week, we left to go back home. It was great because it was
just me and him.*

— HALLIE, DAUGHTER OF MARK BROOKS,
1995 PGA CHAMPION

Few memories bring a brighter glow to a woman's face
than recalling special times she spent with her father
when she was a girl. Sometimes these special times were
like dreams come true, as was the case for Sophia, who
lived her girlhood years in Beirut, Lebanon. She had
dreamed of going to Switzerland, but never really
thought she'd get to go. And then one day, shortly before
her thirteenth birthday, her father, an international
golfing writer and photographer, called her while he was
away on business. She told us, "I remember when the
phone call came. I got on the phone and my dad said,
'You get to come to Switzerland with me!' Not only was

I going to get to go to Switzerland, I was going to get to spend time with my dad, just me and him!

"I flew by myself. They put me in first class, and I was picked up by a ten-person limousine with several golf pros and their wives, my dad, and I. We stayed at a fancy resort, and I had my own elegant room. I spent a week with my dad, on the golf course, with people I knew, going to dinner.

"The highlight of the trip was when he and I attended a birthday dinner for Doug Sanders's fortieth birthday. He was one of the big American golfers at the Swiss Open that year. Because I was educated in a French-Lebanese school in Beirut, I was fluent in French and English, as well as Arabic. So, I translated the birthday speech given by the owner of this very important Swiss hotel where we were dining. I did a simultaneous translation. Then Doug Sanders and everyone gave me a standing ovation!

"I did so many things with my dad that week. I went ice-skating for the first time in my life. I went to all the events with him. Me and my dad. It was really bonding."

For daughters of fathers who travel a great deal for business, taking a trip with their dads can become a lifelong treasured memory. Kimberly told us one of her favorite memories of her father took place when she was twelve, when she accompanied her father to Lisbon for a weeklong business trip. She said, "I felt very grown up, drinking white wine at lunch with him and the Portuguese businessmen. I remember the name of the red Portuguese wine we drank one night on that trip, because dad made a point of saying, 'This is a very good wine.' I remember the kind of gin he drank and the brand of Cuban cigar he chose. I'm not a fan of either gin or cigars, but still, those things are part of my dad for me.

"On the way home, we spent a night and a day in Paris. Dad asked me what souvenir I would like from Paris, and I said I wanted a beret. In France only men wear berets, so we went to a fashionable men's store on the Rue St.-Honoré, and Dad said his daughter would like a beret. I could see the salesmen thinking, 'Who is this American child who wants to buy a beret!' But they measured my head and went to the wall of drawers and opened a drawer full of berets and pulled out one for a fifty-six-centimeter head. I still wear that beret—it will never wear out. Last Christmas, Dad gave me a flier from the hotel where we stayed that night in Paris twenty-five years ago. He treasures that time we spent together, too."

Some men who have travel demands placed upon them have to fight to stay home. Gary told us, "I think that most people don't understand why I don't like to travel. I wake up my daughter at seven A.M. I just touch her. It can be on her head or on her hand. She wakes up and doesn't open her eyes. She doesn't wonder who is there. She just hugs me, serious hugs, from one to ten minutes. I know I won't always get to have that time. But for now, I think this is working just fine for my schedule."

Daughters need not travel internationally to gather fond memories of times shared with their dads. Linda told us, "My dad was a truck driver and he'd take me out with him across the country. When I was really little, I'd beg to go along, but once we got on the road I'd cry so much he'd have to bring me back home. But once I got older, I really enjoyed the trips.

"His eighteen-wheeler had a sleeper in the back, so we'd stay overnight at truck stops and get out and have breakfast. And halfway through the trip we'd stop and get ice cream and coffee. It was a special time that we shared together. It was just him and myself. Our time together."

Not to imply that only travel counts for fond memories of time spent with our dads. Some of the favorite times women described to us revolved around ordinary yet special tasks shared by just the two of them. Teenage April remembered, "When I was a young girl, I went with my dad to help him on our farm. He let me go with him to feed the cows a round bale of hay in the wintertime. I would ride along in the pickup and watch the baby calves run around their mothers. They were rambunctious!

"I also got to help my dad with the combine in harvest. Sometimes he would let me take the wheel and drive while sitting beside him. This year I just learned how to drive the combine by myself. In addition, I helped my dad pick up the round bales in the field and put them on the side of the field. This is where he taught me how to back up a tractor and set the bale down. It doesn't matter what we do together, actually. I am thrilled to be able to go with my daddy without my sisters, just the two of us."

Having special time when a girl can have her dad all to herself is a precious memory for many women. Linda recalled a time when she was between five and seven; her father had a little moped: "Every Sunday, he and I would just take off and go riding out in the country. We lived in England when I was growing up, so we'd just ride all around. I loved spending time with him, just me and him, me on the back of that little moped."

Sharing adventures like Linda did with her dad can leave a lasting impression on a young girl, giving her a love of exploration that lasts a lifetime. Such is the case with Sheena, whose father shared a love of travel with her and her three siblings. She remembered, "My father was a geographer; that was his major in college. He loves to travel, loves the world. So at dinnertime, we'd all sit around the table, and he'd often put a quarter out on the table and say, 'Okay, where's the such-and-such river?' And we'd all take a guess, and he'd say, 'No,' and we'd take out the encyclopedia and look up the river and have this geography lesson. He'd ask, 'Where are the so-and-so mountains?' Often my oldest brother would get the answer.

"Because of my dad's love of geography, we traveled a lot when I was younger. It was wonderful. Four kids, two dogs, and my parents in a VW bus. Many times across the States. Consequently, I've been in all of the states except for Alaska. One of the things he did was take a map of the U.S., laminate it, and frame it. After each car trip he'd take little pins and string and outline our journeys. It was in the kitchen while I was growing up. So after every trip, he'd outline where our journey was, and people would come over and ask, 'What's this?' and we'd say, 'Well, that's where our family's been.'

"That was much, much fun. Most of it was camping. I've seen numerous national parks. We'd drive long distances, and we all had jobs to set up camp when we got there. One year we had three pup tents. My sister and I slept in one, my two brothers in one and my parents in one. It rained almost every night. In pup tents, if you lean against them you get wet. So we spent many nights in the laundry room drying out, sleeping in the car. I have a real love for travel now. I love seeing new places and exploring. It's in my blood."

Not only did daughters collect treasured memories while traveling across the country, but also when they were at home. Delores remembers how much she enjoyed being taken along with her parents when they went out for a social evening. She told us, "My sister was six or seven years older than I, so she was always doing older things. Consequently, it was just me and my mom and dad. Instead of getting a baby-sitter, when they were going over to some friends for dancing and cocktails after dinner, they'd take me along. They'd put some music on and dance, and I was always part of it. They taught me how to dance, and I was really young. We used to dance in the living room, me and Dad."

Christmas can be a time when families create warm and valued memories. Sheena told us, "At Christmastime my parents put our stockings at the end of our beds so that when we woke up in the morning we'd have something to open up. There was a rule that we couldn't go out and see the Christmas tree until everyone was up, the camera was on. Every year there was a new sign, 'Christmas '68.' And so I really enjoyed Christmas when I was younger.

"We'd always play classical Christmas songs. My mother's family had this recipe for nut bread, and to this day we have nut bread. We'd open up one big present and then we'd sit down and eat breakfast. And then the deal was that each person took turns opening up presents. A present deserved an audience. So many times friends from the neighborhood would come to the door asking, 'What'd you get?' and we hadn't even started opening our presents. They were out riding their new skateboards or bikes. As a kid I wanted to get through everything fast. My grandparents were always out for Christmas. As an adult, the last ten years, my grandmother came out until she died last year. My father really put his heart into our Christmas traditions. He was very invested in creating a sense of family."

Not all of the dads and daughters interviewed spoke in the past tense about their special moments together. Many are still in the process of creating treasured memories together. Thirteen-year-old Laura and her father, Darrell, are in the process of creating their special-moment memories. She told us that "by the time I was two years old, my dad (with my mom Beverly's help) taught me to sing my do, re, mi scale. When I was four, my dad and mom inspired me to play an instrument. I chose violin. Before I was six, dad had me recording solos in the studio. Since he worked with a recording company, I spent many hours in the sound room. By the time I was eight, Dad was the minister of music at our church. He started a youth chorus and that meant I had to sing in it!

"As I got older, my dad continued to encourage my music abilities. When I was eleven, I quit playing the violin and started the piano. Dad directed musical productions at our church. This next musical will be the seventh stage production I have done with my dad.

"I love singing. Singing with Dad can be fun, like lying on the beach in the sun. I feel great when he tells me I'm doing good. I know he loves me. So I'm trying to do the best for him now, while he's here, because I know that someday he won't be so near."

Laura proved to us that we don't have to be adults to be wise. Laura realizes that she is currently enjoying a childhood blessed with the presence of a loving father, who nurtures her creativity and talent, a childhood to be savored because, as she realizes, "someday he won't be so near." Equally wise is Abigail, the twelve-year-old daughter of a successful businessman named John. Abigail told us, "I remember when all of my brothers and sisters played Monopoly with Dad. Of course, Daddy won because he's a businessman. When my twin sister, Amanda, and I were little, he used to pick us up and throw us in the air and catch us. But now he can't pick us up because we're too big. He's still a lot of fun. He plays Nintendo with us and watches cartoons with us. I love my Daddy so, so, so, so much! I'll never forget these memories, and I know there are many more to come."

Daughters aren't the only wise ones we interviewed. Toby, Lori's father, also values the memories he is creating with his daughter. He said, "My mother, Lori, and I are born on the same day. I always take my mother and Lori out for their birthdays, just the three of us. And I always take Lori out once a month, so then it's just me and her. Lori's a neat kid. She's a really neat kid."

Dad and daughter alike recall special times together with a lightness of heart. Even in relationships that might be tense at points, when retelling these memories to us, faces brightened and eyes glistened with grateful tears. The special times are the best times we have to remember, and often the way we long to remember or be remembered.

Daddy, the Disciplinarian?

There are three ways to get something done: do it yourself, hire someone, or forbid your kids to do it.

— MONTA CRANE

At the command of my mother he marched me behind the shed to "give that kid a good whacking," then said, "Yell real loud and she'll think I'm spanking you."

— DELPHINE, HOWARD'S DAUGHTER

Ask a father about disciplining his daughter and you might as well sit down for a while, because we found no shortage of opinions on the subject. Toby, an attorney and father of two now-grown daughters, was adamant about the importance of having a father involved in the upbringing of a child. He said, "I think fathers play a different role than mothers. In general, fathers are less nurturing than mothers. And I speak from having handled sixty-five hundred divorce cases and examining more psychologists than you'll ever meet. We serve a different function in a little girl's life, and if you take that father out of the picture, I believe you have a dysfunctional child growing up. I don't think society recognizes that fathers bring something different to the table than mothers.

"Fathers bring responsibility, even a sense of rigidity to a circumstance. And they bring roughhousing to a circumstance. They're more active, they're more physi-

111

cal, they're more involved with sports. Mothers are more nurturing, mothers are more, you know 'clean your room,' 'do this, do that,' 'you need to get into . . .' "

Toby is not alone in his perspective. Many of the fathers we spoke with perceived themselves as the primary disciplinarian, seeing their wives as more tolerant of misbehavior than themselves. Vito told us, "A couple of days before my daughter was planning to go to a dance party, she was very disrespectful of her mother. I told her, 'Ange, if you don't behave, you are not going to this party.' Sure enough, again that afternoon, she lashed out at her mother, and I told her, 'Go upstairs and take off your outfit. You are not going.' Ten minutes later her girlfriend's mother came to pick her up. The mother said, 'Please, let me take her.' I said, 'No, she has to go upstairs. She has to learn.' "

Then Vito added a very important statement. He said, "It about killed me to do it." Even though fathers may feel it's their job to be the "bad cop" of the parental pair, when we dug beneath the surface with many of these fathers, we found that there was a tender spot inside.

Mark confessed to us how badly he feels sometimes after he's disciplined his daughter, Madison: "Sometimes I want to make her be perfect and I fail to realize she is three. I am sometimes so stubborn, even if I know I should back up and do it another way, I continue. For example, I told Madison she had to pick up all her toys before she could get another toy out. Instead of praising her and saying, 'You did pretty good there, just pick up those other couple of things,' I usually go, 'Madison, you didn't do what I told you.' Then later on at night when she's sleeping, I ask myself, why was I the way I was."

Admitting that one has made a mistake may not be some fathers' strong point, although most daughters seemed to know when their dads felt they had crossed the line. Gina let us in on her way of knowing her dad regretted what he'd done: "Dad always had this way of admitting that he was wrong. He is a very gentle and loving man. But as with all people, he could sometimes get fed up with our behavior and yell or swat us on the bottom and send us to our room. Every single time he would do that, we'd be in our rooms crying, and he would come into the room and rub our backs. Now he would *never* say he was wrong, but he would say, 'Now your mean ol' dad loves you even though he might not always show it.' That was his way of saying he was sorry for losing it."

In fact, the more we talked with fathers about discipline, the more stories we heard that contradicted the notion that dads were indeed the strong disciplinarians they made themselves out to be. Dixon told us that he found it much harder to maintain a firm stance with his daughter than he did with his son. He said, "With a son, you feel like you've walked in their shoes. You almost project yourself onto them, rightly or wrongly. But you can't do that with a daughter, because the life experience is different. So, I wind up tolerating more and taking more and forgiving more easily when it's a daughter."

We heard a similar tale from divorced dad Foster, a bodybuilder, who is concerned about nutrition for himself and his family. Consequently, he tries to keep the trips through fast-food restaurants to a minimum. His daughter Hanna, however, has different ideas. He laughed when he told us, "Hanna's like many other kids. She loves McDonald's, and I think that we should only eat at McDonald's a certain number of times during the week. I think we should eat at McDonald's maybe once a weekend, actually. But she knows I like to keep on the go, so she'll say, 'Dad, why can't we just run through McDonald's real quick and just get something and we can eat it along the way?'

"Sometimes when we're planning to sit down and have a little bit more wholesome meal, she will think of food items she wants that aren't available where we are, but are, of course, at McDonald's. That's a good manipulation, but Dad's on top of that one." Smiling, he adds, "I think I've got that one handled pretty good."

"But still, on Friday nights when her mother drops her off to see me for the weekend, and she hasn't had dinner, I'll ask her, 'Hanna, what'll you want for dinner?' and just about ninety-nine percent of the time, it's a McDonald's Happy Meal." In fact, he heads the car toward McDonald's before she has to answer, because, he said, "I know that's where we're going."

Pat echoed this sentiment when he admitted to us that his daughter has him wrapped around her little finger. He said, "I am a stockbroker, a businessman, and I work in New York City every day. I deal with tough characters all day long. But all my daughter has to really do to make me weak is smile. That's it. That's how she gets around me, at nine years old, when other really important smart businessmen cannot fool me, she has me behind the eight ball. The reason probably is I want her to have everything and be completely happy. Those feelings, granted, are not particularly practical, but do manage to rule many times when they shouldn't."

Pat is like the majority of fathers we met, realizing that this little female creature exercises enormous power at times. Alex described how Tiffany, his eleven-year-old daughter, "is the one who is the worst, or the best, in terms of being able to get her way. She just comes up and goes 'please Dad, please Daddy, please, you love me so much. Please Dad, you know you want to. Please,' and I would let that go. She's so cute, I didn't want to say no. I believe I could have, I just didn't want to." Yeah, sure, Alex, we believe you.

Not that we daughters are unaware of our manipulations. Speaking for many of us, Linda confessed, "Oh yeah, I have him wrapped around my finger. Forever, I will. When I was younger, I would give him the lip. The old boo-boo lip. I'd say, 'Oh Dad,' if there was something I didn't want to do. I could talk him out of it, even if it was something like, 'You gotta eat your dinner.' I'd give him the boo-boo lip and say, 'Dad, don't make me eat it, come on, please.' It works, to this day, it works."

For those who don't know the boo-boo lip, Linda explained, "The boo-boo is where my lip, my bottom lip, goes way down and kind of quivers. And I get these sad eyes. I give a look like, 'You better give me my way, or I will just die.' And then I guess he figures it's just easier to give in than stand his ground."

When the boo-boo lip fails, another approach daughters have taken is to evoke a particular nickname, as reported by Romaine. She let us in on her secret weapon, called "Sweetie pie." She said, "As long as I can remember, my dad always called me his 'sweetie pie.' After two boys, he seemed to have a soft spot for my feminine ways! One day, however, when I was about three, I must have been testing this feeling of fondness toward me. In frustration, he turned to me and said, 'Romaine, if you do that one more time, I'm going to spank you!!!' I quickly ran out of the room, not wanting to hang around to test my ability to resist temptation or his ability to follow through with his threat!

"In a few minutes, though, I softly tiptoed back into the room, climbed into his lap, and asked, 'Daddy, am I your sweetie pie?' To which he replied, 'Yes, honey, you know you are.' Then I looked into his eyes with all the sweetness I could muster and said, 'You don't spank Sweetie pies, do you, Daddy?' From that day on, he never spanked me again!"

When a young girl cannot get her way with her dad using her own wiles, she may look around for an even more powerful female presence — the grandmother. Dale observed that even though his daughter Nya is only three years old, she's already good at wrapping him around her little finger. He said, "She always knows how far to go. She's a smart girl. She's always testing her perimeters, she knows how far to push and still get what she wants.

"I try to be a strong disciplinarian, and then my mom laughs at me, 'You're so strict, you need to lighten up.' I stand there thinking, 'This is definitely *not* the woman who raised my sister and me. You know, there's a different set of rules.'

"But even though my mom thinks I'm too tough, my daughter still gets her way most of the time. Once I told her she couldn't have something, so she went to ask her mom for it. Her mom said she was supposed to ask me, but Grandma, my mom, came over and made sure she got her way. She realized that my mom had more power than my wife and I!

"What's a dad to do? Nothing. The child knows how to dial her grandmother. I have respect for my mother. You know the saying, *If Mama ain't happy, ain't nobody happy.* No matter how big you get or how old you get, you still respect your mom. It comes down to the fact: Mama has automatic override."

However, we talked to one dad, Brian, who didn't go for the manipulation technique from any of his daughters. He has three, Amanda, Shelby, and Ashley. He told us, "I decided that I wanted all of my girls to get what they wanted by asking for it. They either got it because it was the right and good thing for them, or not. No amount of pouting or whining works with me. I am very consistent on this. I believe it's hard enough out there in life without teaching them that using feminine wiles will get you anywhere. I want them to understand that being a woman you have the inner strength to do whatever you need to do without having to manipulate anyone for it. Obviously, you can manipulate, and they certainly give it a good go," he said smiling. "But I teach them that the stronger way to behave is to earn whatever you achieve without making yourself a manipulating little girl. I have three very happy and secure daughters. They are very different personalities, but they are very happy in who they are."

Instructions, rules, occasional punishment, and development all come into play when exercising the fine art of disciplining with love. In the same breath that magic word "control" pops up. As interviewers, and as daughters, we have not been able to decide where the control actually rests. Somehow, in the course of this special bond, more often than not, the charm of the daughter's love and her desires have encouraged control to accidentally slip off the dad's broad shoulders, and around her little finger.

You Should See My Daughter, the Athlete!

I was not close to my father, but he was very special to me. Whenever I did something as a little girl — learn to swim or act in the school play, for instance — he was fabulous. There would be this certain look in his eyes. It made me feel great.

— DIANE KEATON

It doesn't matter what I do, he wants me to do it with a good attitude. He always says, "You can do it." Even if it's running or playing hard, he wants me to do my best.

— AMANDA, BRIAN'S DAUGHTER

Girls who were athletic were once considered tomboys. We were expected to sit quietly in our dresses, legs together, and watch while the boys got to play all the fun games. A few girls were allowed to be cheerleaders and jump around some, but by and large, sports were for boys, and looking pretty was our job. Lynn tells how this perspective shaped her when she was a young girl.

She said, "I had two older brothers, Billy and Joe. They were five and seven years older, respectively. When they would be boxing with those big red gloves, I would want to learn, too. They finally gave in and taught me. Both of them thought little skinny Lynn looked so cute with those big leather boxing gloves on her minuscule little hands. I'm sure I did, too!

"By the time I was nine or so, that boxing came in

really handy. We had moved across the tracks to the nice side of town. In my neighborhood, there were only boys. I was the only girl. So, if I wanted to play, it was with boys. I could fight, run faster, and do wheelies on my bike just as good as the boys.

"Every Christmas when Christmas trees were thrown away, me and my 'guyfriends' would ride around gathering them up. There were three little 'clubs' in the neighborhood and we would have these wars with the tree limbs. Those trees were dead, so when the pine needles would hit our winter coats, they would go flying and make this cool sound. When they hit your hands or face, they would sting! Oh mama, they would sting.

"One day after winning the war, I came home. I walked in the door feeling gloriously happy, as my buddies and I had won over both clubs. My dad and mom both said at the same time, 'What happened?' I told them about the war. They both felt I had lost the battle, as my face and hands were nicked in about fifty places.

"My dad then congratulated me for winning. My mom promptly let us both know that she didn't feel I should be congratulated. My dad just said, 'Hey, if she's gonna be a tomboy, she might as well be the best tomboy in the neighborhood!'

"I was happy inside and sad that day. Happy because he accepted me as I was and sad because I was my daddy's little girl in my mind. I didn't want to be his little tomboy. I think it was soon after that I began to have crushes on boys and having slumber parties with new-found girlfriends. Actually, I have always wondered if that was part of dad's psychological plan."

Now, fortunately, these stereotypes are fading and it's possible to be both daddy's little girl and athletic at the same time. Vito told us that his daughter, Ange, "is the boy I don't have. She's very daring, adventurous. I let her run with everything she wants to do. As rough and tough as she is, when it comes nighttime, she's supersensitive. She hugs and kisses before she goes to sleep. She looks forward to having me bring her to school every day. That's when it's just us.

"Two years ago I took her snow skiing. She's very athletic. She does Rollerblading and plays softball with the boys in the street. She got all geared up. The beginner line to learn how to ski was very long and she didn't want to wait. So, I was showing her how to ski. It was comical at first, you know, falling down and laughing when you are learning. Then I had to let her go by herself. I waited anxiously at the bottom. Then I see her coming back on the ski lift, by herself, her skis swaying. I thought, 'Look how much confidence this kid of mine has.' Sure enough, next time she is coming back on the ski lift a second time with two other girls, and they skied the whole day. Then she wanted to go down the advanced hill.

"I told her she had to be careful, but she was determined. Of course, she fell and got bruised. Then she came back and had hurt her nose. My wife cleaned it up . . . and she was gone again. At the age of four she had already had stitches from being so daring."

Gary told us how his daughter, Carrie Ann, demonstrated an uncanny ability for gymnastics at a very early age. He said, "She would always jump off the couches, off the bed, always turning flips. People who haven't seen her for years say, 'Are you still doing gymnastics?' Because she was so small and petite and agile, it was something that came so easily to her. She had two older brothers who were also gymnasts, so they could kind of help her learn some of the tricks. I built her a little bar to swing on when she was just very physical in that respect.

"The other night we watched an old family video, and we saw where she turned a flip, and we were all just hooting, because she was so tiny and she could just flip. It was almost instantaneous, it was so quick."

It is now in fashion for a father to feel proud of his daughter's athletic abilities. Joe told us about his daughter Tonie's accomplishments: "Tonie has been a real spark from the word go. She seemed to be one of those kind of people who has a strong personality. She had to fight the pressure of her four siblings as being the baby. She's hyperdriven with superior intelligence, very competitive, and wants to win in every situation. When she doesn't win, she redoubles her efforts to win the next time. She seems to have a real clear mind and learns things fast and easy. She looks at something and understands it easily, whereas the rest of us have to learn it.

"She asked me how she could become the best. I told her the only way to win was to outlast the other team members. They were faster, because they were littler. She had to develop endurance. I told her that during the off season she had to train harder. She had to run two to five miles every day, and do stairs. That's exactly what she did, too.

"Now, she's the top player in the high school. She made seventeen points alone in one game, which everyone considered amazing. She is now being looked at by coaches of colleges, and they are videotaping her games for scholarships. All of this is because of her wonderful, consistent desire to be the best. I am so proud of her."

With the addition of a national women's basketball league, women Olympic stars from skating to gymnastics, and women athletes commanding high dollar figures for commercial endorsements, we are seeing more than ever before how important encouragement from daddies of athletic girls can be. Previously, natural talent in many women was left untapped. Isn't it delightful that as a culture it is becoming more acceptable for daddies to respond at an athletic event, "Wow! Wait until you see my daughter, she's incredible!"

What Do You Mean, You Want a Cat? And Other Pet Stories

Our perfect companions never have fewer than four feet.

— COLETTE

Little girls often love pets of all kinds, shapes, and sizes, and they usually pressure their dads into letting them keep a variety of birds, cats, dogs, turtles, frogs, and fish. Gary told us his daughter, Carrie Ann, asked for her first kitten when she was about seven years old. Gary was not altogether thrilled at the prospect of having a cat around the house. He said, "I was not really a cat person. I was always geared more toward dogs. So I put it off by telling her she should pray about it and 'if Jesus wants you to have a kitty you'll get a cat.' I thought I was off the hook.

"At that time we were living in Nashville, but I was commuting to Chicago. My wife called me in Chicago one afternoon and said, 'You'll never guess what happened. The neighbor's cat had a litter, and he brought over this little white kitten.' He knew that we had kids and thought that we might enjoy having it. We hadn't talked to him, so he didn't know anything about our deal. I thought, 'Oh man, now I'm really in deep.'

"When I got home, I had to let her keep the kitten, because as far as she was concerned, she'd gotten a clear answer to prayer! She prays and out of nowhere this guy delivers one to the door. I was hoping we'd find a way to rid ourselves of this new pet, but we ended up keeping him. I couldn't take him away. That cat brought huge smiles to her."

Mark's daughter, Madison, got her first pet from Paw-Paw, her grandfather who had gotten all of his grandchildren bunny rabbits. He said, "It was cute at first and fun to be around. Little Bunny Foo Foo (that was its name, no kidding) started to get bigger and stronger legs. It became increasingly harder for Madison to hold him. It was also more and more work for my wife, Shannon, and I to change the pen and keep it clean.

"So, Little Bunny Foo Foo got traded in for a guinea pig. Once again, when he was little he was fun to hold. But the guinea pig had a bad habit of nipping at her fingers. As the guinea pig grew, again it got harder to hold and was biting harder.

"The next trade was better. It was traded for a larger Barbie doll. She cried all the way to the pet store. She said her guinea pig would miss its mommy! I didn't let her go into the pet store. So she said her good-bye and told this crazy guinea pig, that she hadn't held in two months, that she loved him and would miss him. She cried for about an hour. Then we came home and ordered Baby Katalyn, her new doll, and all was forgiven. Occasionally, she will say, 'I miss little Bunny Foo Foo and I wonder how he's doing.'"

While some fathers merely tolerate their daughters' pets, other dads and daughters bond over their mutual love for animals. Sheena recalled some of the most tender moments she had with her father: "He and I shared a love for animals. When our first dog died, I was thirteen or fourteen years old. Her name was Tess. She was half cocker, half doxy, blonde hair, and she was a wonderful dog. She died of cancer. My dad and I buried her in the front yard. The two of us just sobbed. There was a strong connection. All my siblings are animal lovers, and we got it from my father.

"We had a pet squirrel named Rascal that I grew up with for ten years. My brother pulled it out of a nest while we were on one of our trips. My parents tried to put it back in the nest but the mother rejected her and threw her back out. So we brought her home, and my parents called the vet, and they were told to put it in quarantine for six weeks. We got up all through the night and fed her with an eyedropper. My dad was in charge of that. Rascal became this phenomenal pet. Dad built a cage for her outside, but she was inside every day. He'd go out in the morning and bring her into the bathroom while he was showering and shaving. He would bring in a cup full of elbow macaroni, and she'd take it out of the cup and put it in her pouches, and then go to some corner in the bathroom and try to empty out her pouches, and then cover it up. She'd nestle into the towels. We'd walk around, and she'd crawl down your shirt to your belt line and sleep there for hours. We let her run around the rooms.

"Even though my father and I have had problems in

recent years, I still treasure those memories, those sweet moments when I see him caring for our animals with love and kindness."

Daddies take a lead in teaching their daughters how to treat animals. Whether it's how to feed or care, groom or just how to love the animal of their choice, little girls look up to and watch their daddies for pet values. So, when that question, the inevitable question, about pets rears it smelly little head, know that for a daughter it has emotional impact far outlasting that particular pet.

My Dad Isn't Perfect,
But That's Okay

Dads show off. Sadly, dads also fall off, through, and under.

— PETER GRAY

*Dads don't need to be tall and broad-shouldered and handsome
and clever. Love makes them so.*

— PAM BROWN

*We start out imitating the heroes — Bogart, Cagney, Eastwood,
the outlaws and the rogues who make their own rules. Then
along come the children, and nothing else is ever the same.
Suddenly Mr. I'll-Handle-This is wearing a Flintstones cap
and reaching under the couch for some stray peas. Suddenly the
man who would be the Duke has oatmeal on his shoes.*

— HUGH O'NEIL

When we're little girls, there's no one on earth like our
daddies! We are certain that our dads are the best, the
strongest, the wisest, the kindest there is. As we grow
older, however, we begin to see their humanity, their
flaws, and their shortcomings. For some, this realization
comes as a shock. Other little girls take it in stride. But
nearly all of the women we interviewed had to face the
fact, somewhere along the way, that their dads weren't
perfect, but that was okay. No one needs to be perfect to
be loved.

Jessica resisted this realization, and almost lost her

then best girlfriend over insisting that, indeed, her dad was the only perfect dad in the world. She told us, "In the second grade, I remember talking with my girlfriend Donna about her dad. She was bragging how her dad did all these wonderful things for her. I wanted to say that my dad was even better than hers. Since you can't do better than perfect, I said, 'Well, my dad is perfect!' She said, 'No one is perfect!' I responded, 'Well, my dad *is perfect!*' And that was that! I completely ignored that he wasn't there for me all the time, but in my eyes, he was my dad, and he fit that bill for me. Donna and I didn't talk for a couple of days, but as is often the case for girls that age, we soon made up and became best friends again."

As girls grow into teenagers and then into women, we usually expect their fathers to be exhausted by their daughters' growing pains. However, it's not always the child who is the trouble maker in the family. Hope told us about her dad's antics with a tone of sweet chagrin: "It seems, in most families, that the kids do things that horrify the parents. But in my family, it was my dad who always horrified us kids. He was a person who really didn't care what other people thought of him, including us at times, and we were at the age of being embarrassed by everything out of the ordinary.

"He would order two cups of coffee in restaurants and then proceed to pour them back and forth and into the saucers to cool them down. When the meal was finished he'd wash his hands in his water glass. He'd then 'tip' the waitress with a huge replica of a dollar bill he'd had printed as a joke — giving them a 'big tip.'

"He'd wear wild color clothing way before it was 'cool' to do so, and he'd mix plaids and stripes, if he liked both of them, whether they were even the same color tones. In later years he even decided to cut his own hair. He could never do the back properly, and it would be a choppy mess. He couldn't see it, so he didn't care. He probably wouldn't have cared even if he could see it.

"We had a CB radio in the car and he would pull into a strange town and announce 'Dairy Queen call — where is the Dairy Queen?' We'd be so embarrassed — but we did enjoy eating the ice cream. He'd stop at every general store and drag us all inside to 'talk to the local folk.' Since we were shy, this was a real trial to us. When traveling in Canada he'd force me to talk French to the people since he didn't understand it himself and I'd taken French in school. I thoroughly hated this and was a beet-red color the entire conversation. He also told us that the first three rows of all crops were open to the public and had us gather bags of fruit everywhere we went. I was quite old before I found out this wasn't true.

"Yet he had his good side, too. He taught us that people were more important than things. Even if we crunched up the car he didn't care as long as we weren't hurt. One time while shopping I accidentally left my purse in the shopping cart and went into a dressing room. When I returned my purse was gone. Later the purse was found in the garbage can outside the store, but all the money was missing. My dad replaced all the money, telling me that he could afford to lose it more than I could. Again showing me that I was more important than money.

"My father was a brilliant inventor and patented many things that the world uses now. The patents expired and others actually put the products into production. He would mostly lose interest in an invention once he had solved the puzzle of it. If he had been a better marketer we could have been rich. Before he died he gave some of his best inventions away, saying that the world had need of these things. Again, people were more important to him than the money. My dad was a complex character, and we had a complex relationship, but I will always miss him and the wisdom that I gleaned from him."

Discovering one's father is human isn't all bad. Accepting our dads' flaws can help us be more accepting of our own shortcomings and those of others we love. Thirteen-year-old Chelsea learned this lesson from her father, Brad, through humorous circumstances. She told us, "I remember one time we were playing Trivial Pursuit and he was trying to give a clue for the Jetsons, but he started singing the Jetsons' lyrics to the Flintstones' tune. He sang, 'Meet the Jetsons. Meet the Jetsons.' And we all started laughing at him.

"At first he got defensive and argued that he was singing the right song. Eventually, though, he had to own up to it, because we were merciless. I admire how my dad admits when he's wrong. I've learned from his example that once you realize you're wrong, you should admit it. It helps me see that I'm not always right about everything. That's an important life lesson.

"And I've learned to trust what my dad says more because he can admit when he's made a mistake. Whenever he's forgotten to do something that he's promised or he's run out of time, he'll always come back and apologize. And usually he'll make it up to me in some way. I've learned that when you promise someone that you'll do something for them, you really have got to let them know if you've let them down. Admit it. You can't just blow people off."

Chelsea, although young in years, is already becoming a wise woman, as she recognizes that no one is perfect. And certainly if fathers and daughters alike are willing to own up to their imperfections, it creates an atmosphere of acceptance and forgiveness. After all, isn't that what we're really looking for anyway?

Oh, No. She's Behind the Wheel!

I've learned that wherever I go, the world's worst drivers have followed me there.

— A 29-YEAR-OLD DAUGHTER

Lynn has a confession to make about her first day behind the wheel, which was also the day of her first car accident! She admitted, "I would be the perfect example for the court to verify that a person should be at least sixteen to have their license. I got my license on my fourteenth birthday in Texas. In fact, I got it early that morning, and I picked up my best girlfriend, Nita, so we could get a hamburger at the local Whataburger. We were laughing and having the best time. We both ordered hamburgers, fries, and Cokes.

"As I went to get in my mom's brand-new Delta 88, Nita and I decided to have a milk shake to go. I decided to continue the fun and hilarity of this joyous day by waiting until Nita was ordering those milk shakes and speeding off and leaving her stranded for a few minutes. I started the car. She looked back and smiled. I put the car in reverse waiting for the perfect time for her not to be able to get out to catch me. She began her order; I hit the pedal. I thought I had looked back to clear the way, but I forgot one thing. There was a huge, round cement block with a light pole attached directly in my blind spot.

"I hit that cement block so hard it crunched that

back end like I was wadding up a piece of paper. It was a loud boom! Everyone in the restaurant came out. Nita started laughing. I started crying. I was in *major* trouble. The manager said that, since it was on private property, and there was barely a dent in that stupid cement block, to go on home. What was I going to do? My mom and dad, I was sure, were going to kill me . . . but worse than that, take my much-coveted driver's license away.

"Then Nita got scared when she realized that her parents could associate her with my mistake, and bingo, 'No driver's license for her.' She began to cry with me! I was driving the four miles home, and the rear bumper, which was barely hanging on, was banging, bumping, screeching the loudest sounds. With each sound I would cry out harder and so would Nita.

"When we finally got to my house, I pulled the car into the garage and closed the garage door. I didn't want to look at it and I didn't want Mom or Dad to see it first thing when they drove up. I then walked into the house and called my dad. I knew better than to call Mom. When I heard his voice, "Hi baby, what's going on!" I just lost it. I became hysterical. In the middle of my overdramatic wailing, I got across to him I had wrecked the car. He said he'd be right there and hung up.

"What I didn't know was that Daddy thought I was hurt. He thought his little girl was hurt and had *left* the scene of an accident and he was going to have a lot of cleanup, not the least of which was a car. He was home in about four minutes. He walked in the door as white as a sheet.

"I began to scream, crying again, when I saw him. Finally, he got me calmed down to get the facts. First, he was happy that I wasn't hurt. He was so relieved when he found out I hadn't left the scene of an accident or that no one had been maimed or killed. Then he wanted to see Mom's new car.

"When I opened up the garage door, he turned to me and said, 'Honey, this is what we have insurance for. This situation could have been way worse. I am so glad my baby is not hurt, no one is dead, and you enjoyed your Whataburger today.' He then asked for my driver's license. I thought it would be forever before I saw that license again.

"Instead, he showed me how to deal responsibly with the insurance company. This information came in handy for the next five wrecks I was in . . . all of which were not my fault! Honestly, they weren't. I was hit from behind each time, when I was either stopped or preparing to stop."

Fathers, with daughters on the road, all shudder a bit at the thought of receiving a phone call that begins, "Dad, I've been in an accident." Thomas told about his daughter Celeste, who "totaled three cars — two Ford Mustangs and her mother's BMW. By the time she totaled the BMW in 1993, it was old hat to us. I was in Austin and couldn't get back up here. She had flipped the car and was in the hospital, but it was too late for me to get a flight out of Austin. Fortunately, she wasn't hurt badly and got out of the hospital before I could get back to town.

"It was a very different story with her first two wrecks. She was really upset. At first, she was concerned more about her car than she was about herself or anything else. And the car's replaceable. But explaining that to a kid who's just received a car, her first car, is very difficult. I talked to her, and she came through okay. Now she's a pretty good driver, but she learned the hard way."

Many of the fathers we interviewed told us that when they've received a phone call about an accident, their first worry is about their daughters' well-being. John tells about a recent auto accident that happened to Tiffani, his eldest daughter. "She called me on my cell phone and I was out of my office immediately. I got to her totaled car before the police. I couldn't believe it. Here was my little girl safe, by the grace of God. She's almost twenty, and five feet eleven inches, but at times like that she's still my little girl who needs my help. She literally spun 180 degrees in the middle of a major Dallas freeway and was hit head-on by a van. She moved from the far left to the far right lane. Then stopped on the shoulder of the road. The tie-rod broke, and the back wheel locked. It was a miracle she was alive. She only had airbag burns out of the deal. When I realized how close she came to losing her life, we sat down right then in my car, said a prayer, and thanked God."

Dads weren't the only ones who told us "daddy-daughter" car stories. Most women we talked with had a number of tales related to cars, usually around maintenance and repair. Kendra told us, "We lived in Arizona when I was growing up. I moved into my first apartment, and I had my own car. I had gone to a convenience store one night and the car broke down, so I had to leave it there overnight. My dad was able to repair anything, anywhere, so I called him the next day to help me.

"It was probably 118 degrees out there and my dad really sweats a lot. In that heat, he got in my car and worked and worked and worked, just dripping from sweat, and he fixed my car. It was very hard for me to watch, so hard for me to have to ask him to do this for me. He was the only one who could help me. When the car started running, we were both pleased. It was rewarding to count on him that way."

Wanting to make sure their daughters are safe while on the road, dads often "go the extra mile" to keep their daughters' cars in running condition. With fondness in her voice, Peggy recalled, "When I was in college, my mother got it in her head that I needed a car. And so, the next week, my father bought a very, very old car and fixed it up for me, had it painted. It was not by any means an expensive, fancy car, or one that you could take out of town, but he worked very hard on the car, so that I could have something to drive around town. You couldn't get it to drive over thirty-five miles per hour; then the front end would probably shake off. I kept that car until I got married."

Lynn has another story about how her father helped teach her to drive: "After getting an A in driver's education, I was off to take the test. I passed with flying colors. I attributed my expertise to my driving instructor, who was a disciplined but fair teacher, and my daddy. My dad used to take me out to the oil field and let me drive on the dirt roads. He taught me how to spin out on the gravel and keep the car in my control. Over and over again we practiced going from the paved road onto the gravel, so I could handle the car's different reactions.

"This really came in handy recently when I was on my way to Lexington, Kentucky, to see my little nieces and nephew, Chelsea, Claire, and Evan. I was 'making time,' as my daddy used to say. I was driving an Oldsmobile Aurora and decided to stop off at a Dairy Queen for the relished Diet Coke. It had just started to mist as I was exiting at a 180-degree circle. The car began to spin out. The left side of the road was at an angle, so that there was about a five-foot drop, and the right side of the road went into a hole. It was amazing how those lessons, so long ago taught to me by my daddy, came flooding back. I knew exactly what to do instinctively to make that car behave.

"It did scare me, though, as I hadn't used those skills for at least ten years. I got to the Dairy Queen, which was right by the exit, and a gentleman got out of his truck to ask me if I was okay. After assuring him I was fine, he told me he was behind me and was sure I was going to career off that sloped road into a very serious accident. He had already picked up his cell phone to dial 911 for assistance. He couldn't believe that I got the car back in control. Thanks to daddy and God's angels, I can write about it today."

It seems by nature the majority of daughters do not consider themselves mechanically inclined. (For those of you who are, please don't be offended. In fact, we are quite jealous of your talents!) However, we often look to our daddies for guidance in the car arena. We count on them to help us maneuver through what we consider a haze of mechanical language that plagues us from the beginning of wanting to drive a car to the day we hang up our drivers' licenses. Thank you, dads, for helping, rescuing, and putting up with us as we endeavor to successfully operate in the car field.

Dad to the Rescue!

*I could not point to any need in childhood as strong
as that for a father's protection.*

— SIGMUND FREUD

*A dad is a man haunted by death, fears, anxieties. But who
seems to his children the haven from all harm. And who makes
them certain that whatever happens — it will all come out right.*

— CLARA ORTEGA

Scary things can happen to little girls (and big ones as
well). When we're little, we most definitely need our
dads to protect us as best they can from dangerous people and situations. Once we're grown and out on our
own, we need to know how to protect ourselves. It's not
that easy these days, but we learn to trust our natural
instincts and recall those lessons taught to us by our
fathers.

Dixon is like many fathers who are concerned for
their daughters' safety. He confided, "I have the same
apprehensions that any father might have about physical
dangers of the world. I have served on the City Council
here in Arlington, Texas, and there've been some poignant moments dealing with the Amber Haggerman
murder. A little girl who was taken off her bicycle in
broad daylight and was found several days later, dead.
The murder has yet to be solved. It's like the Polly Klaas
story. In fact, Polly Klaas's father has been here and

involved in the discussions on how to keep this thing from happening again. It's scary. I guess it brings you to the realization of how quickly your life can change. My wife and I do our best to make sure that all of our children are not put in dangerous situations. However, you can't ensure that completely, so there's some apprehension and some scary moments.

"As my daughter grows older, I have to face that I can't live her life for her. I'm getting more comfortable with the fact that I can't control everything. I've always been the one who has wanted power over my destiny, my surroundings, and those who are around me. Hopefully, I'm learning not to be too overbearing, because she's going to have to make her own way in life. A lot of what you learn in life is by trial and error, and you've got to, within reason, make your own mistakes, and then find a way to move forward. But I think you also need to know your parents are an anchor and a base to come back to, so I make sure that she knows that her mother and I are there for her."

Having that home base gives a daughter confidence to go out and try things on her own. Mistakes will be made, accidents will happen. Knowing that you've got Dad still there for you when the going gets tough can make all the difference, as Linda found out when she first moved out of the house when she was eighteen. She said, "I wanted to see what living on my own would be like. I had a job at the time as a waitress, and I thought that's all I needed, so I moved out. Maybe two weeks or so later, and I go,

'Oh my God, I don't have money for the rent!!' So, I called Daddy.

"I asked, 'Dad, do you think you could loan me some money?' That money didn't last long, and I didn't like living by myself, so I decided to move back home. Before I moved, I wanted to get my security deposit from my apartment and the landlady wouldn't give it to me. I called my dad, and I said, 'Dad, you've gotta help me out by talking to this lady and making her give me my security deposit.'

"The landlady's house was about a mile from our place, so he went there with me and said, 'My daughter . . . ,' then he looked at the lady and said, 'Hey, I went to high school with you!' She went, 'Oh, hi Greg, how are you?' I felt like an idiot. But I asked him, 'Can you still get my money for me?' And he did. She was nice now, because she knew him. But it was sort of embarrassing because he was going up there to say, 'I want my daughter to have her money back.' He extended himself on my behalf that day when I am sure he would have preferred not to greet an old friend with that request."

Not only do daughters benefit from the protection they receive from their dads, but dads also get a kick out of helping their daughters, a sense of satisfaction that they've been "good fathers." Joe recalled that one of his favorite moments as a father was a special time when he helped his daughter, Desiree, with a personal problem during her first week at junior high school. "Desiree came home with a stern but worried look on her face, threw down her books, then started to pace back and forth. Then she asked to talk to me alone. We went to a room at the back of the house where I painted and worked on sculptures.

"At first she rambled on about many small things before she could get to the subject that bothered her. She slowly explained that she wished to do well in this new school but had a bad time because she was the new kid on the block. A few of the kids teased her, and she had tried to handle the problem through the correct chain of command, by talking to her teacher, but was met with a total lack of interest. Desiree was very upset but had maintained control, refusing to cry. Bit by bit I could see a slow burn in her eyes and knew an explosion was just under the surface; this problem must be put to rest, fast. She wanted to learn self-defense, and she stated she had a large score to settle at school. She definitely wanted her pound of flesh very soon.

"I explained that she really had two problems with a common thread. Both were caused by a bad school environment where ambivalence was the norm. This new word surprised her, because she did not know its meaning, so I explained. I then helped her understand the power of words to overcome problems. I told her, to solve a problem she must first fully understand the whole picture and all its parts. Then, and only then, would a solution be found. I told her she could not expect anyone at school to help her with this problem. She must solve it and then maintain control for herself. What was called for was a creative plan to regain control of her personal space, then keep herself in control in the face of new attacks.

"Two kids were able to harass her because the school staff was not doing their job in the school halls. Desiree wanted to 'destroy' the kids and 'spit in the eye of the deadhead teacher.' But now she saw that, while words could hurt, words could also defuse and control conversations in life. I taught her how to shield herself with well-chosen words. We outlined a plan in which she could always gain control of this problem. To master this ongoing problem she must rise above the negative people and keep them at arms' reach with the right words spoken at the right moment. I helped her understand that she had no way of changing people, but she could control the moment.

"She increased her verbal skills with larger words to counter the small hurtful words of others. She understood she was in a war of words she could win starting now. She must always express herself in a more intelligent way when the battle was started by others. *Never* attack, only deflect words with words.

"The next encounter was very, very different in its outcome. The following day the two kids approached her with many silly, hurtful comments, then waited for her wounded reaction. Desiree slowly turned with a poised air and calmly stated, 'Withdraw, you mindless, moronic neophytes,' then turned away from two stunned, speech-less boys and went cheerfully on her merry way.

"After one more encounter, these two bullies avoided Desiree like spoiled bubblegum. The teacher was like-wise handled in the classroom, when Desiree was put on the spot by the teacher to make a point. She looked the teacher in the eye, assumed a poised air, waited a full ten seconds, then used words well beyond her years; this ended all future problems.

"This was a turning point in her life. She was now in full control of herself and could deal with those who would try to hurt her. As her father I found a jewel in Desiree; she became a happy, fulfilled person who still shines today."

"To protect" is defined in Webster's dictionary as "to defend from attack or loss; shield." In the event that fathers are not present the moment their daughters need protection, many dads can take great consolation in the fact that they have given wise counsel so their daughters can protect themselves. Dads and daughters alike can share a sense of confidence that this sometimes danger-ous world can be managed.

"Not With My Daughter, You Won't"
And Other Boy-Related Dramas

The thing to remember about fathers is, they're men.

— PHYLLIS McGINLEY

Michael, the father of eight-year-old Jacque, has it all figured out. He told us, "I'm not worried about my daughter when she gets old enough to date. I've already gotten her to promise she won't go out with anyone until she's thirty-five." We hated to break it to him, but we doubt that this is one promise his daughter will be able, or willing, to keep.

Fathers seem to start worrying about the "other man" in their daughters' lives almost as soon as they are born, and certainly once they start off to school. Vito told us about his reaction when his nine-year-old started telling him about a boy she'd just met. He said, "I thought it was cute the first day she came home telling me about a young boy she had a crush on. But it also got me thinking about how I will influence her choice of men. I thought about the loving care I give my daughter, and that some-day some guy is going to come along and I will be secondary. So I want to be the best possible person, role model, so she will choose a man similar to myself. That's what I work toward every single day, to be a better person for her."

Once a boy shows up for a date, dads have been

known to "have a man-to-man talk" with this scared young man, to make sure all goes well. Alice recalled a time when she went out with a guy and she'd gotten sick while on the date: "The young man had not brought me home when I had asked him to. We went ahead to the movie when I wanted to go home. When my dad found out, the next time that guy came over my dad gave him a good lecture on taking me home when I requested. I just about died when he started in on that guy, but I was also grateful. He was protective like that."

Since dads were once young men, they seem to know more about what's lurking in their minds than we women might. Luann gives her dad credit for saving her from a serious mistake, when she was under the spell of her "first real love. My dad had a sixth sense, a homing device, a protective instinct given by God. I was incredibly in love with this young man and considered getting married without my parents' permission. There wasn't anything tangible that they could put their fingers on, but my dad felt that this guy was a control freak. My dad called him a 'guru.' He said, 'You are going to end up barefoot and pregnant.' He knew that in my heart *that* was not what I wanted for my life.

"My dad said, 'if you will just go to college for one year as one last thing for us, then, you can do anything you want.' So, I agreed to go to college for one year to honor them. I sure didn't want to, but they had been supportive of me and I felt it was the right thing to do. That summer, I didn't get to see my boyfriend the whole summer. I remember crying so hard I actually thought I would die."

"Then one of my good girlfriends called me a couple of months into college and told me he had been dating another girl all summer behind my back, and they had gotten married. All of the things, it turned out, that I ended up doing in my life, the girl he married had wanted to do, and she ended up barefoot and pregnant, just like my dad predicted!"

While a father may want to protect his daughter from serious mistakes, there doesn't seem to be a fool-proof way to accomplish this. Even the wisest of fathers can't predict the future of a love affair. Fathers come in handy, not only to help us make sound decisions regarding men, but also to comfort us when things go awry. Debbie told us how her parents helped her cope with her very first broken heart. She said, "Picture a dismal night of Christmas Eve slammed into a metal gray morning of Christmas 1977. That was the color of my heart. I had lost my first love.

"I greeted my family on Christmas morning with bloodshot, puffy eyes, a hollow stomach from not eating, and nervous muscles from lack of sleep. The morning of all hope was dawning, while I felt my life was over. Love letters found. From him. Written to her. Not to me.

"Had I been able to keep my mouth shut, it's possible the day could have progressed rather simply, disguised in phony joy. But I did open my mouth and my family heard a seething, sassy, evil-spirited girl, flinging all manner of venom. Mom had only asked me to help set the table.

"I pushed my family away. I could not let them in. They would never understand. I had lost my first love! And I made my parents suffer for it.

"By late morning, it was time to open presents. I only wanted solace in the dark cave of my blankets. There was no holy justice, there was no glory of Christmas. Christmas reeked! He was gone. For good. He was happy in the love of another. I had lost my true love!

"I only remember opening one gift that Christmas. A small box which held a tree ornament. It was from Santa. But I knew it was from Mom. I knew her handwriting. The ornament was a wooden plane, bright yellow, red propeller. Tied to the tail was a note: 'We know you want to fly far, far away,' was all it said.

"I suddenly bawled. Bricks crumbled from my fortifications, exposing a punctured heart. They knew! Instinctively, I dragged myself to my father, who sat in a nearby chair. I crawled into his lap and he held me close to his chest. Mom knew. Pops knew. They understood. I hadn't been in his lap since I was six. I was twenty-five years old and all five feet eight inches of me was hunched in my father's lap. I wept and he held me and I bled and he rocked me and I gasped and he enfolded me into his life-giving embrace. My father had the uncanny sense of knowing what to say to whom at a given moment. He knew exactly what to say to me. He never said one word."

In the attempt to protect daughters from broken hearts and young men with dubious intentions, some fathers act behind the scenes. Lynn told us how her dad, and one of her brothers, kept her protected without her knowledge when she was in high school: "I am the baby of the family and the only daughter. I was allowed to start dating at the age of sixteen. I was a baton twirler. I especially liked the boys in the percussion section, although I did try to date every officer in the band, to give them a fair chance.

"I began to notice that I would go on a date, have a great time, and then that was it. The guy would be really nice to me, but wouldn't ask me out again, even if I strongly hinted that I was interested. Growing up in the South, a good girl would never ask a guy out. Eventually, I would just give up and move on, since there were plenty of cute guys in our school of twelve hundred.

"Then one day, I happened to be coming around a corner and heard some of the guys talking. My name came up, and I stopped dead in my tracks, waiting to hear what was being said. I knew it was eavesdropping but I couldn't help myself.

"Ted was telling Jim about my brother Bill and how tough he was. In our high school they had YMCA groups that were kind of like fraternities and sororities. Bill, who had already graduated, was renowned for being in the toughest but coolest YMCA guys' group. My brother had put the word out that a guy who dated me twice would be in trouble with him! Also, I was 'hands off.' No affection of any kind, except hand holding! I was furious when I found out and went home resolving on the way to get even with my brother. Dad did ground him for two weeks. Many years later I found out from Bill that Dad was the one who told him to do what he did, and he actually never was truly grounded. Now it is funny, but it sure wasn't back then."

While "putting the word out" for boys to beware works for some fathers, others take a more practical approach, realizing that teenage girls have a natural, healthy need for social contact. Loraine told us, "Most of my life, I was well behaved. But when I was in the fifth grade we moved to Texas from England. Both of my parents are English, and we moved here for my dad's work. The entire family was traumatized, me especially. All the kids laughed at me for having this formal English accent.

"Because of the pressures, I became a hell-raising teenager, and my mother really couldn't handle the situation. She decided the best thing for me was to go off to some boarding school in England. So my dad took me to look at schools.

"We visited one that my mother really wanted me to attend. It had a thirty-foot fence around the school, and my father asked the principal, 'Do any of the girls date boys here?'

"The school official said, 'Well, you know, they have a dance about once a month at the boy's school down the street.' My father was smart enough to realize that this was not good for me. Even though my mother said, 'Take her, get her out of here,' he knew that this school wasn't going to work. It would simply make me more rebellious." Loraine's dad demonstrated his acceptance of her appropriate need to date by making sure she had ample opportunity to meet boys her age.

Loraine's father took this a step further, when he made a decision about his daughter's budding sexuality. Loraine told us, "I was a bad teenager. I'll admit that. When I was sixteen, my mother found my birth control pills, and took them away. But I always thought my dad was real smart, 'cause he gave them back to me. He said to my mom, 'If she has them, then she obviously has a reason for having them, and if she knows she needs them, then it's fine with me.' My mother said, 'Oh, don't give them to her,' like that was really gonna stop me."

Loraine's father had accepted the fact that, in the end, a girl will make her own decisions about the boys she dates, and what she does on those dates. But this is not a truth most fathers willingly accept. Even for fathers who feel their daughters will make wise choices, there is usually a pang of sadness, concern, and loss when they watch them drive off with their dates. Gary described his feelings as his daughter was preparing for her prom: "The timing of this interview is interesting because my daughter's prom is tomorrow night. She just got asked, and she accepted without discussing it with me or her mother. We've not had any hard and fast rules, like 'no dating until you're sixteen,' or something like that. We just discuss things together and then decide as we go along.

"Well, this time she decided on her own without talking to us, and I didn't like that at all. She bought a dress and some shoes, and I haven't actually met this guy yet. We do know his family, but I don't really know the kid. I told her, 'I think it's really fine that you go. I'm really happy that you got asked to go. But before you make a commitment like that, you need to talk it over with me and Mom so we can all decide, so we all know what's going on.'

"She said, 'It's too late to say no.' And I said, 'No, it's literally not too late for your dad to say no.' But after talking it over, my wife and I felt good about her choice, and we want to continually reinforce as many positive decisions as possible.

"I hope I have done my job up to this point, because it's time for me to trust her judgment. And we really do trust her. Nobody is infallible. There will probably be mistakes made along the way, so I want to keep the communication going."

But what's a dad to do when communication breaks down? Jack told us what he did when his daughter, Melanie, didn't make the best choice. In fact, when she put herself in serious danger, he told us, "She was only fifteen and didn't have a driver's license. Regardless, she and this guy took off with one of our cars and headed out of state toward New Mexico.

"I went down to a coffeehouse here in town where I

knew she hung out. And of course nobody talked, so I offered small bribes and, amazingly, some people began to remember. They said, 'Oh yeah, she took off with this guy to go to New Mexico.' Well, there wasn't much I could do if she was on the road, but supposedly, they were coming back soon. So, I offered a really sizable bribe — one hundred dollars — to the first person who saw Melanie and called me.

"While she was on the road, Melanie hit a deer and pretty much trashed this brand-new car. And that's not all. She gave her sister's driver's license number to the highway patrol. She had memorized the thing. So her older sister now has an accident record. She then talked the cop out of arresting her. She finally showed up back in Dallas. I knew she was in town because I was sitting at a fund-raiser with my tux on and my pager went off several times within a few seconds. I knew there had been a Melanie sighting. I called the first number, and it was the guy behind the coffee bar at this teenage hangout.

"So I turned to a friend of mine who works out with weights and is a pretty muscular guy, and I said, 'I need your help. Go to your house, put on a tight shirt, because we have to go downtown to pick up my daughter.' I had no idea what to expect. I didn't know the kid she had gone off with, or if they had picked up drugs, or what I was getting myself into. I was a little nervous about this, well, maybe more than just a little bit.

"I ran to my house, changed clothes, and asked my

friend to meet me. As we drove downtown, I called another friend on my cell phone, a big guy with twenty-inch biceps and a fifty-inch chest and looks about as mean as a junkyard dog. We all met at the coffeehouse about the same time. The three of us walked into this place, these two guys walking behind me looking like muscle men. I walked in and the place was crowded, but it parted like the Red Sea. I walked right to the bar and said, 'Can you tell me where my daughter is?' and the bartender said, 'She just left.' So I asked about the young man that she had been with.

"He pointed to a kid who was literally about twenty inches from me sitting at the bar, so I turned around and tapped him on the shoulder. He turned around, and I said, 'I'd like to introduce you to your worst nightmare.' His eyes got about as big as quarters, because he saw the other two gentlemen that were standing with me. I got a little bit over the edge. Dad was an upset person. I asked him where he'd been, what he'd done, really grilling him. Even though it was crowded, people moved away from us. He told me he hadn't done anything to Melanie, and I said, 'Young man, my daughter had better not end up pregnant.' His eyes got about as big as silver dollars. The poor kid was about 135 pounds dripping wet and maybe about five foot seven or eight. Then I turned around and walked out and went to my ex-wife's house to pick up my daughter. She has lived with me ever since.

"I found out later that an ex-cop owns the coffeehouse and he was behind me all the way. He wanted to put the fear of God into her. When they had come in he said, 'Melanie, you'd better get home,' and she asked why. He said, 'Well, your dad is coming.' She wasn't scared, and said, 'Well, that's just my dad.' He said, 'No no no. I had your dad checked out and he is one of the five people in Dallas that you wouldn't want to upset.' This poor kid she was with didn't know what was happening to him. But Melanie wasn't scared at all. She knew all three of us guys are just pussycats, but all the boy saw were these really rough guys, so he thought his life was over. Last I heard, he was crossing two or three borders.

"From that day on, I realized that there wasn't anything I wouldn't do for my daughters. I am not a violent guy. I'm really not. But the thought of someone taking advantage of my little girl was very upsetting to me. I was so afraid that that kid had done something to my daughter that I was over the edge a little bit. I don't think I'm alone in this. I think a lot of fathers have that in them. Not men in general, but fathers do."

It doesn't matter if their daughters are six or sixteen, fathers have an innate desire to want to keep them safe from other males who might want their little precious ones as "prey." Knowing how men think, dads can sometimes assume the worst of a young male suitor. We found that the biggest challenge facing protective fathers was not other males — but the strong wills of their own daughters and the fact that, at some point, these dads had to let their little girls grow up into women with minds of their own.

Where Is the Little Girl
I Once Knew?

The hardest moment in fatherhood is probably more of a constant — the fact that she's grown so fast and that time seems to fly by. I guess that's what all parents go through.

— DIXON, ALISON'S FATHER

One day, when the children are grown, dads mean to drop the mask and take up where they left off. It comes as a shock to discover they have lost twenty years or so — and they are balding. And the children tower above them, and pat them on the head.

— CLARA ORTEGA

When is the moment a little girl becomes a young woman? When does a father lose her?

Gary described a recent experience in which he realized his child had become a woman. "The family had all driven in from Chicago that night, and we needed to stop at the grocery store for some milk for breakfast the next day. So we brought everybody home and unloaded the car first. While we were unloading, Carrie Ann, my fifteen-year-old daughter, showered and put on a dress she had purchased from an outlet mall on the trip. She came down the stairs, wearing a casual long, black dress. Her hair was wet from being in the shower, kind of combed back in a sexy model look. She looked great. I mean, she really had a striking look.

"She wanted to go to the store with me. It was around ten-thirty P.M., so off we went. I didn't think much of it until I noticed people's reaction to us in the checkout line. The cash registers were manned by kids her age. They looked at her and then at me like, 'What is that dirty old man doing with that nice young girl?' I felt really ill at ease. Carrie Ann was totally oblivious. She feels comfortable with me and I with her, just like she does with her mom.

"We got out of the store and I started to relax, when a police car drove by. We were carrying a couple of grocery bags. Then I thought, "They might think we were taking them back to some apartment or some hotel. I really felt uncomfortable then. I wanted to say really loudly, 'You know, oh sweet daughter, dear daughter, would you please open the car door?' Anything to let them know that was my daughter and not a young lover.

"I realized that when a girl turns into a young lady, it actually happens in a relatively short amount of time. It's not only a physical metamorphosis, but also an emotional thing that happens. It's the way they carry themselves. As young women they have a whole different look and a different countenance. All of a sudden they are not just someone's kid. They have become a young adult, a young woman."

Fathers aren't the only ones who miss the special bond between a dad and his young daughter. Teenage girls and adult women we interviewed talked with a sad fondness of their childhood relationships with their dads.

Thirteen-year-old Chelsea told us that her dad, Brad, doesn't spend as much time with her now that she's a teenager. She said, "He used to play games with me. If I wanted, he would come in and play Barbies with me. And he'd let me comb his hair. I would take ponytail holders and try to put as many in his head as I possibly could."

Carmen's mother, Mary Ellen, shared a similar story about special times she and her father shared when she was a little girl. Mary Ellen recalled, "My father had a full head of gorgeous hair, naturally curly hair. Some afternoons he would take a nap on the couch and he'd let me put rollers in his hair. When he got up, I'd comb out his hair and it would stick out, full and funny-looking. I still smile when I remember how he looked. I loved playing with his hair."

Crystal sent us an essay she authored about her dad. She wrote, "No one can deny that there is a special bond between a father and his daughter. I can remember back when I was little, my dad would ask me, 'Are you my girl?' I would always reply, 'Yes, Daddy!' That was his little way of asking me if I loved him. Because my dad is the kind of man who never talks about his feelings. That's all right, because all people show their emotions in different ways.

"Reminiscing, I recall a time when I was about five, my daddy took me fishing. I really didn't like fishing that much, but I didn't tell him that. It was something special that we did together. We'd wake up early in the morning to pack the truck. After that was done, we'd get in and start the engine. My daddy would then look down at me and smile and say, 'Are you ready to go, Princess?' Then we would spend the rest of the day at the lake, fishing and swimming. On the way home I would fall asleep in the truck. He would carry me into the house and put me to bed, even though I was awake and just wanted him to carry me.

"My father and I have a special relationship. It changed as I got older, but I know that he still loves me just as much as he did when I was little. I went from asking him, 'Daddy, will you help me ride my bike?' to 'Daddy, can I borrow the car?' And now and then, he will ask me, 'Are you my girl?' I will reply, 'Yes, Daddy!' I love my dad and I will always be his little girl, no matter how old I get."

We may grow older, but few of us outgrow the desire to be our dads' little girls. April echoes this sentiment when she sent us the following essay: " 'I love you, Daddy, because you're so warm and fuzzy!' the little five-year-old girl exclaimed in her childish, innocent manner as she jumped into her father's arms. She buried her face in his chest and cuddled up next to him on that cold Saturday afternoon. The rest of the people in line to get their lunch laughed at how silly the statement sounded. Even her dad laughed. She felt her heart sink as she heard his chuckles. She hadn't meant to be funny. She really *did* love her daddy, and hugging him always gave her a warm feeling inside and she didn't know why.

All her worries evaporated, though, as she looked up into his eyes and saw the tears welling up as he saw her hurt expression. She knew then that Daddy loved his little girl, too.

"Yes, that was me back in the days when I hugged my dad in public, when I told him I loved him regardless of who might laugh, when my daddy was *everything* to me and I was his 'little girl.'

"But things changed. I grew up and entered the 'wonderful world of teenager.' A world where you talk to your parents as little as possible, much less hug them or, God forbid, say the 'L' word when somebody, I mean *anybody,* can hear. A world where you do what you want regardless of what parents say. A world that's not quite so warm and fuzzy. A world where you no longer view yourself as a child. A world I had grown to know too well.

"During the early stages of these years, I fought with my mom a lot. My mom is not one who listens to reason, and I'm not one to listen to her. We argued over the stupidest things almost every day. With the late hours that Dad worked, he often wasn't there to comfort me or come to the rescue.

"I still love my dad very much. I like to talk to him about guys, girlfriends, school, God, anything in general. I quit viewing my father as 'Daddy' and started viewing him as my friend, my *dad.* We got along great, but something seemed to be missing.

"Last year I found that 'something.' It all started when

my mom and I got into another one of our numerous fights, only this time my dad happened to be home. I thought he would stick up for me, back me up, tell my mom to cool down. He didn't, though. Instead, he told *me* not to talk back. I now realize he was trying to prevent the bickering from escalating, but at the time I felt betrayed. I went into a screaming fit, and before I knew it my mom's hand slapped my face. I closed my eyes as I saw her pull back her hand, preparing to hit again, and awaited the blow. Nothing happened. When I opened my eyes, I saw my dad grasping her wrist.

"I ran to my room, bawling my eyes out. My mom and I had never before gotten into a fight that bad. I was just lucky my dad had been there to save me. I became really upset with myself all of a sudden. I couldn't figure out why I had acted so horribly. Especially after all my parents had done for me, all my dad had done. It was making me sick just thinking about it. Then I heard a knock on the door. I tried to say something, but the knot that was swelling up in my throat prevented me.

"We didn't speak a word, I just cried on his shoulder. 'I'm sorry,' he said after a long silence. He didn't need to say any more. I knew what he meant. I finally realized what was missing, and I was sorry, too. I had been missing my 'daddy.' As I felt his tear land on my shoulder I once again became that little five-year-old girl. 'Do you know why I love you, Daddy?' I stuttered between sobs.

'Because you're so warm and fuzzy.' I meant it, too, only this time I was talking about his heart."

Even when there are no problems in the home, teenage girls, like Hillary, are often caught between the worlds of girlhood and womanhood, one minute demanding the rights of an adult and the next melting into "Daddy's little girl." Mason Cooley observed, "An adolescent is both an impulsive child and a self-starting adult." It's hard to know which one, the child or the adult, you are talking to at any moment; the change can be rapid and catches many a parent off guard.

Allen described how he tries to keep up with the rapid role changes of his teenage daughter, who lives out of state with his ex-wife. He said, "My daughter is now working fourteen hours on the weekends at a photocopying place, taking orders for copies as well as being cashier. The other day she called me and moaned about how she wants to rent Snoopy videos, stay in her pajamas, and watch cartoons all day. She told me that to make her life perfect, I need to make our 'colored pancakes.' We just add color to the pancake mix, creating bowls with different colors, and voilà — multi-colored pancake stacks. She whined, "Daddy, I don't wanna grow up and work. I want to stay a kid." It kills me, because half of me wants her to stay my little girl and the other half knows that it's my responsibility as her dad to guide her and help her grow up. It's a dilemma."

It's hard to know who suffers the most from this transition, dad or daughter, since both long to move forward while neither wants to give up the past "warm and fuzzy" connection. So, bumbling and mumbling, while their daughters are crying and sighing, Dads try to help their daughters mature, while secretly wondering, "Where is the little girl I once knew?"

Section Three

Adult to
Adult

How My Dad Influenced
My Choice of Career

When I was little my dad named me "goobaby." This year we went on a business appointment, and I am the president of Emphasis Music. The lady reached out to shake my hand and said, "It's nice to meet you, 'goobaby,' your dad has told me all about you." That, of course, helps to build all kinds of credibility in a business deal.

— LAURA, STUART'S DAUGHTER

Not to minimize the role mothers play in our choice of careers, we've found that fathers often play a significant role in the way their daughters learn to deal with the "outside" world. This fatherly influence can start back when we are little girls, in the ways our dads reacted to our performance at school, how they supported or discouraged our exploration of our talents, and if they delighted or scoffed at us when we told them what we "wanted to be" when we grew up.

Laura attributes her strong sense of competence, in part, to the way her father participated in her schooling. She told us, "I was very active in school, but my dad was even more active than I. He was very proud of me. I felt a sense of approval, love, and self-worth from that which has helped me go on as an adult. It's funny, every now and then he will ask me about someone from that time. He'll say, 'Have you talked to Melanie recently?' This will be a person I have had no contact with for twenty years. It's interesting that this was an important phase not only to me, but also to him.

"Dad has taught me persistence and the value of working hard. He taught me how to dream dreams and how possible opportunities are. I know his interest played a big role in my feeling capable of creating my own music business and succeeding at it."

Ronni credits her admiration for her father as a strong influence on her choice of career: "My dad was a junior high school math and science teacher, and later a counselor and an administrator. I have a brother and a sister and all three of us have become schoolteachers. I've been teaching now for nineteen years, and am now a resource teacher. He has had a tremendous impact on us all.

"I remember how, when I was a young girl, he'd take me to school functions where he worked. They used to have all-school skating parties where he'd chaperone. I got the chance to see how the kids liked and admired my dad, see how teachers would interact with him.

"Also, we'd run into students of his at the mall. They'd come up and say, 'Hi!' clearly glad to see him. Kids and adults would come up to me and say, 'Your dad is just the best!' I'm still amazed at the fact that my dad would always know their names. Even when he was principal, he'd learn the names of almost every kid in the school. And because of my dad's example, I make sure I know my students' names by the end of the first day of school.

"None of us went into teaching for the money! Back

when my dad was working, teachers weren't paid year round, so the summer months were very lean ones. But I wanted to make a difference in somebody's life like that. I saw that helping others that way was so rewarding. I knew I would get back the satisfaction of being able to affect a change. That was worth the sacrifices."

Some fathers affect their daughters, not because of the support they give, but because the daughters turn a negative situation into a positive. Alana told us that her father was abusive when she was a girl, and badgered her emotionally whenever she made the slightest mistake. She said, "My father was German and very strict. He taught me that perfection was attainable, and it wasn't until I grew up that I realized that it wasn't. I lived under that cloud of perfectionism for years.

"But I remember one wonderful moment in my family kitchen, I asked him about his life. He described the farm that he grew up on in New Jersey, and this really hard man dissolved into a marshmallow as he talked about farming and animals. I knew he had a knack for growing things because he used to experiment with fruit trees in the back, grafting them. We had one tree that was half peach and half nectarine. He'd make walls out of adobe by digging up earth and mixing it with hay, and I got that from him. I'm very much an earthy person. And I love to grow things, and I love to create things from nothing.

"As we talked that afternoon, my father taught me how to make my first omelette. Even though on my first try I burned the heck out of that pan, this time he was gentle with me. I'm sure that experience had an impact on me, because now I am a caterer. I love to prepare food. To me, cooking is a way to show love. I have a really strong attachment to food in a lot of different ways. I love to cook for people, and do parties."

Kimberly, who also had a troubled relationship with her father, attributes her choice of career to his influence; she's a writer and editor. She said, "My first job was secretarial work in my dad's office during summers. By the time I had to get a job on my own, I knew all about how offices work, how to do correspondence, how to correct the English written by engineers who worked for Dad, and how to spell terms like 'state-of-the-art' that were not taught at school. I knew from that experience that I had an ability with words, and that knowledge encouraged me in my dream to become a writer."

Eddie, father of Sasha and Chiara, feels that he influenced both of his daughters in their choices of careers. He told us, "I think Sasha got her aggressiveness from me, because growing up, I was very aggressive myself. I was a fighter. I practiced the martial arts. I boxed the Golden Gloves. Sasha grew up, more or less, like a tomboy, always a very challenging young lady who liked to fight and do boys' things. So, it makes sense to me now that she'd choose to become an inner-city police officer.

"When she first told me, I was shocked. In fact, she suspected I'd be a bit upset, so she told everyone else in the family before she told me. I actually heard about it first from my sister, and I thought she was joking. Sasha was very hesitant in telling me; that's why I was, probably, the last to know.

"It's been hard for me to understand why she'd want to work downtown. It's terrifying, confused, and rough in the city, and the fact that she's so excited about it kind of makes me wonder if she really knows what she's getting into. However, I keep her in my prayers and I wish her the best, because I'm not the type of dad who's out to try to turn a child around or change a child's mind or make them decide what they want to do, whatever they want to do.

"Chiara is twenty-two now and she's in school to become a CPA. Chiara's always been the brains in the family. She's always been the one who wanted to have both book and street knowledge. However, she has a little street, but she's a lot book. She loves books, she loves to read and write, and she likes to talk a lot.

"One of my favorite stories about us was one Christmas, I believe it was 1985, when we were all together for Christmas and exchanging gifts and having fun and laughing and singing and doing family things. We played Scrabble, and she was coming up with words that were not in the dictionary or in the Scrabble book. But she just made it clear to us that these words did in fact exist, these were words. And they weren't. And all through the whole game, she just did that, she fought and fought, trying to make us believe they were words. So it wound up being a pretty fun night.

"That told me that she is a very strong-minded young girl who won't take no for an answer. She's a fighter, like me. I think Chiara got the brains from me, because I'm now a writer and a public speaker. Chiara is the one who I have chosen, once I have become successful in my business, to become my CPA. So it's come full circle. I've influenced her, and now her life and her behavior will play a key role in what I'm trying to do. So, I would say that she's having a great impact on me."

The key words here are "mutual influence." We daughters make our own decisions based on our own talents. However, many of us would not have the careers we have today if our dads had not been there to affect our sense of self, positively or negatively.

Squaring Off With Dad

Just do what we say, Dad, and no one will get hurt.
— ASHLEY AND ALYSE, BOB'S DAUGHTERS

At some time or another, most women stand nose-to-nose with their fathers and declare their independence. Sometimes this confrontation occurs in adolescence, other times well into adulthood, when a daughter lets it be known that she is no longer going along with her father's program.

Alana told us, "I've given my dad a lot of food for thought. In fact, my weight has always been an issue with my father. I've had a lot of eating disorders, and he would criticize me. I remember the year that I decided I wasn't going to be afraid of my father anymore, and we went up to see him at Christmas, and, sure enough, he reached out and grabbed my spare tire. And I took his hand and I said, 'Dad, there is so much more to me than that.' His eyes got *sooo* big. But I had to reclaim that power from my dad. At the same time, I wanted to deal with him in a loving way, as opposed to the hatred that I grew up with from him.

"That night, before I went to bed, I crawled up in his lap. I stayed there while he stroked my hair. I gave him a kiss goodnight. It was really healing. I think sometimes we don't know how to heal, unless somebody presents it to us first, so I gave him the opportunity, and he did respond."

Esther squared off with her dad when she came home during a break from college. She said, "He was very prejudiced, and I didn't know any black people until I went to college. But there I made several close friends and had to change my narrow views. I erased the word 'nigger' from my vocabulary.

"During the visit, my dad used that word, and I told him not to say that anymore. He said, 'It's my house, and I'll use whatever word I want to.' I said, 'It's my ears, and I won't listen to it. I'll leave. You have a choice. You can use this word in your house, whenever you want to, and I won't be here, or you can spend some time with your daughter. It's up to you.' And so he never said it around me from that day on. He'd say it around everyone else, but he'd never say it around me."

As in Esther's situation, squaring off with our dads comes after we've had some physical or emotional distance, giving us the chance to establish our own sense of self and our own values. Sometimes, because our fathers represent such powerful forces in our lives, we need the support of someone else to help us draw the line and stand our ground. Such is the case of Sandy, who gathered courage to stand up to her father after she watched her husband square off with him first.

She told us, "After a couple of years of marriage, my husband began to stand up to my father. The first time was when my father wanted us to be dishonest about the warranty on the transmission in our car. My father had given me the car years before, and we had a pattern of turning to him when the car broke down. My dad wanted us to bring the car down to where he lived and, even though the warranty was out, my dad planned to lie about it so he could get it fixed for free.

"I overheard a phone conversation between Don and my dad. Don said, 'I'm not going to do that. It's not honest.' My father wanted to do something in an under-handed way. Don has been a man of truth from the get-go, from day one, and sniffs out any kind of decep-tion. His radar goes 'bing!' and he won't go along with anything like that. If the warranty is out, it's out. He's not going to try to talk his way through, or pretend anything. He deals with life the way it is.

"This infuriated my father. Don rose to the occasion and basically met my father head-to-head, as opposed to avoiding the situation. He got angry back. It was the first time Don let himself be a man against another man. It was really important for me, but it also scared me, too. Here was my father and my husband going at it. It was on an issue that was a moral issue and around the car. It was very charged.

"Whoever controlled the car had a direct line to me. It was very tense. We eventually gave the car back to my parents, because they needed it. We said we'd return the car if they would open an account and put some money into it for Alexis. So my father put a thousand dollars in the bank for our daughter. Perfect. He bought it for two thousand dollars and bought it back for one thousand dollars. But that control issue and that 'I know better' and 'I'm going to do it my way' and 'I'm going to save money on it' are all issues that were very, very full of tension for me. I can talk about it today without it going into my gut. A few years ago, if I talked about this, I'd need to take a nap right now."

As Sandy realigned her attachment from her father to her husband, she gained the strength to stand up to her dad when Don was not around. She recalled, "Just about three months ago we went to an amusement park. As we drove up, Dad said, 'We'll get you a pass and Alexis is free.' I said, 'What's the age cutoff for small children?' He said, 'She's turning two next week.'

"I felt my stomach turn. I said, 'What do you mean, she's turning two next week? She's going to be two and a half soon.' So he started to get aggravated. I said, 'No. I don't want to lie about her birthday. If the limit is two and under, great. If it's two and above . . .' He got really mad and said, 'Then you can pay for her.' This is from her grandfather who absolutely adores her. I must have touched him in that place of shame. My father has a lot of shame. I believe it comes from his father shaming him a lot.

"So I said, 'Okay, I will.' And I used Don for strength. I said, 'Dad, if Don were in the car we would pay for her.' So he said, 'Then you can.' My mom jumped all over my dad and said, 'You should be ashamed of yourself.' It was like six bucks or whatever, a very minimal amount for Alexis. So there's this huge tension in the car. My dad got real quiet, and I was so proud of myself. I feel like I stood up for myself and what I believe in, right in the moment. I got to experience the embarrassment, the hot anger, but I just said it the way it was.

"As it turned out, the cutoff for small children was three and under, so the whole issue was moot. He hadn't even checked it out, but he was already preparing in his mind that she was going to go in for free. He didn't bother to look. It relieved the tension, but it showed me that he didn't care what the facts were. He'd already decided he wasn't going to pay for a child. If I hadn't squared off with him, I would have walked around all day long feeling ashamed to be related to this man who wouldn't pay for his granddaughter, and ashamed of myself for not having stood up for the truth. I felt so good about addressing the issue then and there, not letting it go. I avoided dealing with my dad's displeasure while I was growing up, and now, as an adult woman, I was ready to take that on."

It is definitely hard to stand up to your dad. You have to cross that invisible line between "Daddy's girl" and woman. Fathers we have interviewed told us there is a sense of pride when the daughter draws her line. Of course, all those involved, especially when it's in the heat of anger, would rather not have to deal with this passage. But it's a special part of becoming a woman, making the transition in your heart from little girl. And in the same breath, it's a letting go, or at least, allowing a little slack in the string of protection that the father feels. If his daughter can stand up to him, she'll have a good chance of being okay in her dealings with anyone else who may come her way.

He Could Always Make Me Laugh

If you're going to be able to look back on something and laugh about it, you might as well laugh about it now.

— MARIE OSMOND

Few things bond two people together like shared laughter, and dads and daughters are no exception. Memories that bring smiles to our faces are those we treasure our whole life through.

Laura told us that she and her father share an offbeat sense of humor that few others, if any, understand. She said, "To me, what he does seems so very funny, while others just roll their eyes. For example, he sang the tune, 'Boomer Sooner' and made up this word 'poody-doody' and started singing it over and over. I thought it was hilarious and the thought still makes me laugh. Others think it's silly. Sometimes it's so unfunny it's really not funny, but it's pretty rare for me to think that about his form of silliness."

Alice and her father share a love of playing tricks on each other. She recalled, "He had this pair of over-sized dice that I liked. I asked if I could have them, and he said, 'No.' So, I took them anyway and put them in my apartment where he could see them. Then he would take them back and put them up in his place where I could see them, and we would never say a word about it to each other. I just thought it was funny how we teased each other with those silent jokes."

One doesn't have to be all grown up to appreciate a fun moment between dad and daughter. Teenager Chelsea told us about a time recently when she and her dad, Brad, shared a good laugh: "My dad and I have the same sense of offbeat humor. One time my dad, me, and my sister were at the airport going to visit my grandma when she was sick. My mom was already out here with my brother. My dad went to the other side of the airport for something, and when he came back he told me that he ran into Miss America. We were going, 'Oh, yeah. Right.' He kept talking about how she had seen him with us, and how she told him he was such a good dad, so patient and all. I said, 'Right, Dad. Miss America really told you that you were a great father.'

"When we got out of the airport, this beautiful lady in a limo drove by and waved. She called out, 'Bye Brad!' to my father. I stood there with my mouth wide open. It was Miss America!"

Gina told us about a joke she and her father, Vyron, shared while she was a little girl. She said, "I had this thing with my dad every single night from when I was three to when I was eight. I had told him one night that I never wanted to grow up and get married and leave him. So, he said, 'OK, we will just keep you from growing up.'

"Each night I would go into his room and say, 'OK, Dad. It's time.' He then would push on my head to keep me from growing up. Now at thirty-three we joke about this, and I say to him, 'You didn't know this would really work did you?' I still live at home and am not married."

While laughter can come from lighthearted fun, humor can also help make a tragic situation more bearable. Carmen tells how her father's sense of humor helped her get through the stressful time when he broke his leg. Carmen said, "I take after my father in that we are both very strong-willed. At one point he got it into his mind that he needed to leave the hospital and go home. He tried repeatedly to get out of bed, which was forbidden because he had a special cast on his leg that could not bear his weight. I said out loud, 'How am I ever going to keep this man in bed?' He grinned up at me from the bed and said, 'Don't think it's likely.'

I said, laughing, 'Dad, you should go into stand-up.' He said, 'I couldn't be a stand-up comic. Maybe a lean-to comic, but not a stand-up.'

Mary Lynn shares an interesting adventure in humor that probably doesn't occur in today's world: "There was a crash in the stock market in 1929 and Daddy harvested a lot of cotton bales. Cotton went down and he lost our two farms. I went to work right after I got out of high school and worked about six months. And dad got two trucks and we came to Lubbock, Texas, from East Texas. We literally looked like the Beverly Hillbillies.

"My brother, Dale, just older than me, was driving one truck and Dad was driving the other. There was a train running along the track next to us. When the train was going up a hill it would slow down, and when it went down a hill, the train would pass us.

"So Dale and Dad would pretend they were train engineers for hundreds of miles, giving each other the highball sign, as if they were tooting the train whistle. We'd laugh and laugh. That's all it took in those days to keep us interested. We thought moving was this big adventure, because that's the attitude Dad had, when probably it was really hard for him and Mom."

Without laughter, life can be as dry as an old bone. Through good times, or difficult situations, humor lightens our load and bonds us closer together. Especially during crises, humor can be a matter of choice. One can choose to laugh with life, as Mary's and Carmen's fathers did, even during the most stressful times. And the stories that live on, long after the hard times are over, can enrich the relationship between daughter and dad.

"Dad, There's Another Man in My Life"

First and foremost, they are our fathers; and whatever magic we had with them, even if for just a few of our very early years, profoundly affects us for the rest of our lives.

— CYRA MCFADDEN

[M]y father would pick me up and hold me high in the air. He dominated my life as long as he lived, and was the love of my life for many years after he died.

— ELEANOR ROOSEVELT

When Carmen was little, her father told her that any man she brought home would be given a series of IQ and educational tests. (Is that why she's still single today?) She is not the only daughter who worried about what her father would do when meeting her new love. Cynthia told us, "I am the oldest girl and am now in college. When I told my dad I was bringing my first boyfriend home to meet him, his response gave me a cause for alarm. My dad said, 'I am going to be sitting on the front porch waiting with my shotgun!' I couldn't believe that he was saying it, but I was still going to bring Teddy home to meet him.

"Then the day arrived, and we walked up to Dad's house. He wasn't on the porch. There was no shotgun. Teddy was certainly relieved. We walked into his house and found him in front of the television set, and I said,

183

'Hey, where's the shotgun?!' He just kind of waved me off like I had made it up. He and my boyfriend were both a bit leery of each other, but did the manly thing and shook hands. Soon after, they went out on the porch to talk. They have been talking ever since! In fact, they are such good friends I can hardly get in a word edge-wise. It turned out great."

Not all stories flow this nicely, as Gina's experience demonstrated. She told us, "When I was a freshman in college, I met this boy, Matt, who was an upperclassman. I was quite taken with him. Here was a guy who seemed a lot older and more mature, even though it was only a couple of years. He starting liking me and asking me out. I was totally infatuated with him, just thrilled to be dating him. So, Mom and Dad decided to come up to the college and meet him.

"Before they came, I got both of them on the phone. I said, 'Dad, please don't ask him anything to embarrass me.' He said, 'Don't worry, I'll just ask him if he has a résumé or what his real intentions are with my daughter.'

"I was a little panicked and begged my mother, 'Please tell Dad not to say anything that will embarrass me.' I just didn't want Dad to scare him off, since we hadn't decided to date exclusively. So my mom said to my dad, 'Now dear, don't you embarrass Gina.' I got off the phone, hoping for the best.

"The next day, they pulled up in front of my dorm where Matt and I were sitting. I walked over and hugged them and I made the introductions. Dad stuck out his hand and said, 'Nice to meet you, Matt.' I held my breath. He continued, 'Now, did Gina tell you I needed a résumé before you could date her anymore?' Matt said, 'Well, no sir, she didn't.'

"I died. Mom looked at Dad with looks that could kill. We were going to get lunch, and I invited him, but Matt declined. I just knew Dad had scared him off. We were eating lunch and I had one of my best girlfriends, Kim, with us. Dad joked around, saying that Matt didn't take it seriously, but I was furious with Daddy. He tried all kinds of jokes to get me out of the anger. By the end of lunch, he felt awful and said, 'Where's the nearest mall?'

"Dad knew I had wanted cowgirl boots for a while. My girlfriend thought it was great, I would at least get some boots out of the deal. Dad took me and bought me some boots (which Matt totally loved, because he was a country boy). Matt and my dad got along really well from that day forward. Dad had not scared him off, even if he did get me angry."

Dads everywhere must believe it's their duty, not only to protect their daughters, but to humiliate them as well! Cheyenne shared her experience: "When I still lived at home, I was always nervous bringing guys around my dad. He was like, 'That's *my* daughter!' I was such a daddy's girl. One day it had been raining, and a bunch of us were going out. I had just washed my hair when the electricity went off. My hair was wet and I was in a hurry. So, I called my boyfriend and asked him to run over and pick me up so I could go to his house and dry my hair.

"Well, my boyfriend drove up and tooted his horn, which I didn't even think about, and ran out to hop in the car. My dad stormed out of the house, furious. He screamed, 'No daughter of mine is going out with a guy who just honks for her!' I mean, Dad was pulling me out of the car and I was screaming, holding on to the steering wheel. My boyfriend, shocked at first, knew better than to interfere and just laughed nervously. Dad won, of course, and I went back in the house. After things cooled down, I ended up taking the car over to my boyfriend's house, did my hair, and went out to eat. Needless to say, I didn't end up marrying the guy."

Jewel was a young sixteen when she introduced her boyfriend to her dad: "When I brought my future husband home to meet Dad, Benjamin already was suspect because he was older, a musician, and had long hair. The first thing Dad said to him was, 'You know, son, I don't really like musicians.' Benjamin didn't fight back and calmly said, 'Well, you know, there's a lot of work involved in being a musician.' That's how it started. It only took about fifteen years, but Daddy and Benjamin have learned how to respect each other."

Introduction to any man that might take your daughter's heart away can be a threatening situation for a dad. Not only is he being watched (or listened to behind closed doors) by a daughter hoping for the best outcome, but he is risking a place forever in history in his daughter's eyes. It's a Hallmark moment that many dads and daughters can now laugh about, and causes a few husbands to cringe still.

Daddies want to make sure their girls end up with the best men possible. Interviewing and threatening with shotguns can be one way, but Dale has his own ideas. He told us, "Most importantly, I want to make sure that my daughter sees how much I love her mom and that I treat her mom with respect. Then she'll have a healthy concept when she's old enough to date. 'Cause if it's up to Daddy, she never will date. I want my child to grow up and be an independent and intelligent young woman, like her mother was when I married her. If she feels good about herself, she'll hopefully make the right decisions."

The Day of the Wedding

Nobody has ever measured, even poets,
how much the heart can hold.

— Zelda Fitzgerald

Most of us women dream about our weddings from the time we are little girls. Picture your ideal wedding and invariably you'll see yourself coming down the aisle on the arm of your father, but looking into the eyes of your husband-to-be. While the notion of "giving the bride away" has perhaps gone out of fashion in these days of political correctness, most daughters long to feel their father's strong arm gently guiding them down the aisle, as a symbol of supporting and blessing them as they begin a new and significant phase in their lives.

Sophia told us that she and her father cried together, right before she walked down the aisle: "I have a wedding picture with that look on both of our faces, like we've just been crying, that tender father-daughter moment — 'this is it.' Even though you can't tell from the picture, I was the one holding him up. He wasn't crying at that moment, but he was incredibly filled with emotion.

"I was smiling — my smile could have broken my face, that's how elated I was. David was singing to me with a nine-person backup. My dad's voice broke when he gave me away. His tears reverse and he gets choked up. He's very tender and very sentimental, but he can't just let it out very often."

Tears often abound at weddings, and fathers can be among the most emotive. Tender feelings can be left unexpressed on a daily basis, but as daughter and daddy start that life-changing walk down the aisle, words of love, long overdue, are often spoken. Jessica described such a moment of tenderness: "When I was two, my dad gave me a little white New Testament Bible, and I kept it all those years. He had inscribed some fatherly wisdom in the front that had meant a lot to me. I had planned on carrying it down the aisle, whether he gave me away or not. Well, when we got alone that wedding day, I showed it to him and told him of my plans. I had never before or since seen him with tears in his eyes, but that day they welled up full."

All women hope for this romantic dreamlike reaction from their fathers on their wedding day. Unfortunately, that is not always the case. Nancy told us how the tension was almost unbearable at her wedding: "As my father was walking me down the aisle with a formal expression on his face, he said, 'You can *still* get out of this. You know this is a mistake!'

"While looking at my beloved Carl smiling, I said, 'Well, Daddy, it's mine to make.'

"Then while we were standing at the reception line, Carl and I holding hands, Dad was being moved along, prodded by my mother's sense of formality. When he approached Carl, he reluctantly offered his hand. He then said, in the most stern tone, 'I believe that my daughter is making a serious mistake.' That's how our married life started. My parents never did really accept our marriage. But, after five kids and many years of married life, you know you are still in love on the way to Wal-Mart."

While most women dream of having their fathers with them on the day of their wedding, sometimes illness or other life stresses can challenge the dream. Dorothy was fearful that her father's cancer would make it impossible for him to participate in "her" day. She recalled, "He'd just been in the hospital for surgery, and I didn't know if he'd be able to make the wedding at all. He was able to get out of the hospital in time, but he had had most of his right hand amputated, and he was really self-conscious about it. They left a finger and his thumb, so that he could hold things, but he wouldn't shake hands with anybody, and he always had his hand in his pocket.

"After the wedding ceremony, we were in the reception line, and he had to shake hands with all these people. And he told me, 'I'm just going to shake with my left hand, 'cause I want to just hide this other hand.' That was certainly fine with me. The whole time he shook hands with all these people and didn't realize it until it was over, that he hadn't kept his right hand in his pocket. All of a sudden he realized it, and it was like, 'Oh.' Quickly he put his hand back in the pocket. It meant a lot to me that he got so involved with greeting everyone, and was so excited about my marriage, that he forgot about being self-conscious about his hand."

Weddings mark the beginning of a new era not only

for daughters, but for daddies too. Bradley told us that he's had some adjusting to do, accepting the fact that both of his little girls are now married: "My oldest daughter has been married for five years, so I know her family and her husband. In fact, she has a daughter herself now.

"The biggest adjustment I'm making now is getting used to the fact that my youngest daughter is married. She just got married at the end of May. I'm trying to learn about her husband. I've only known him for a couple of years. It's tough for me to accept someone's taking my baby away. Even though I know they're happy, it's just a different experience because she is my last one.

"My oldest has been married a while now, so the youngest one getting married has been hard on me. She had been away to college, she lived close enough by so we'd still see her every weekend, when she'd bring home her laundry for us to do. But now that she's married, she doesn't do that anymore. I miss her a lot, because I don't see her every day now.

"I know in my head that this is the right thing for her. Her allegiance is to her husband. That's the way they were taught. Our allegiance goes to our spouse. And the more time passes, the happier I am for her, because I see how happy she is. On her wedding day, she was just aglow, and she still is today. They're so in love with each other, and their happiness makes me happy. I think the more time I spend with them, the closer we get as one larger family."

As the father stands on the steps of the reception hall, with a bill for the wedding in one hand, and perhaps a handkerchief in the other, he knows that his life is forever changed. His little girl is now someone else's wife. The eyes that once gazed at him with admiration, letting him know that she thought he was the greatest man on earth, now look lovingly at another man. It must be a bittersweet moment. His daughter's wedding marks an accomplishment they both have worked hard for. And yet, in reaching his goal, he loses his "one and only" place in his daughter's heart. And for letting go, and for letting us love other men, we daughters thank you.

"She's a Mother and I'm a What . . . Granddad?"

I've learned that children and grandparents are natural allies.
— ANONYMOUS

As we collected stories for this book, we found there was no topic so able to bring a glow to the faces of those we interviewed as that of *grandchildren*. Whether a dad is proudly describing his daughter's expertise at being a mother, or a woman commenting on what a great grandfather her dad has become, there seems to be a lot of affirmation going around.

Foster beamed with pride when looking into the future and predicting what kind of mother five-year-old Hanna, his daughter, will be when she grows up. He told us, "Hanna's going to bring a lot of joy to the world. Hanna's got a real caring spirit, and will be a caretaker in some sort of fashion. I don't know whether she's going be a nurse, or a doctor, or whatever, she will help people. And she'll be a really good mother; she'll be a very good mother.

"I can predict that because her mother's a good mother. She's got a good role model as far as that goes. I respect her mother for that purpose. She wants the best for Hanna. Even though we're not married, we are in sync as parents. We try to stay together with the way we raise her, what her rules and regulations are and how we raise her."

The spiritual principle that teaches that you reap what you sow is holding true for Bradley and his daughter, as he proudly described the way his daughter is parenting her children. He said, "My daughter is a good parent, so I must have taught her something well. My granddaughter loves her mother, my daughter, just like my daughter loved me. It just perpetuates itself. It's just wonderful. I'm really not amazed, because I think I expected it, based on the love that I tried to show to my daughter. This love goes through my daughter to my granddaughter, and you can see it return."

From the time she was a little girl, Dorothy remembers her dad saying, 'You never ever give up on your children, no matter what.' He and my mother didn't get along, I don't know why they ever married. But I can remember my dad saying several different times, 'I can understand how a man could leave his wife, but I don't understand how you could leave your kids.' And that's something that just stuck with me, and the problems that I've had with my kids, that no matter what, I'm still the mother, and that I still love them. He taught me to teach my kids that."

As daughters heap praise upon their fathers in the role of granddad, Peggy told us, "I think that my dad is much more active with his grandchildren than he could have ever been when he was raising us kids. He was so busy working then. But now, he is extremely involved with my kids. He visits my son's basketball games, takes the kids to golf practice, even pays for golf lessons. But it's more than that. He's become a mentor to his two grand-sons. They get together and go horseback riding, and my dad will call me and tell me, 'You know, Tommy's struggling and I gave him a little advice on what I thought was the right thing to do.' He never had time to do all of those things when we were twelve, thirteen years old; he was always at work, and it's kind of nice to see now. There is my dad, the grandfather, becoming a surrogate mentor, the father he always wanted to be."

Not that the mentoring must stop at the grandchild level. Delores told us how her father is actively involved in the lives of his *great*-grandchildren: "When I was a little girl, I'd sit on my father's lap, talking about some-thing, and we'd pretend he was this big monster called 'bullolvus.' We'd just be chatting and all of a sudden, he'd pull his legs apart, and I'd fall down on the floor. I thought it was so funny. I knew it was coming, but I didn't know when. Suddenly, he'd spread his legs and I'd fall through and start laughing. It was really a big hoot. He was so much fun to play with.

"Now my dad plays this game with his great-grandson. My daughter is in school at nights and she will take her two-year-old son, Kevin, over to my sister's from time to time. My sister, who is retired, lives with my dad now. My daughter told me that when she picked up Kevin the other night, he was having this paper fight with Grandpa. Kevin was just howling with laughter. Grandpa was trying to give him a little smack with this little tiny piece of paper and he was smacking Grandpa with this piece of paper; it was really cute. Grandpa was getting a kick out of playing with this little great-grandson of his. He's playing with him the way he used to play with me when I was little. It's great seeing a ninety-some-year-old codger playing with kids. Amazingly enough, we're on the third generation."

Granddads can say things to our children that we, as parents, would never say. Delores is grateful for the help she received from her father when she was raising her teenage daughter. She said, "I was divorced at the time, and raising a teenager alone is hard. My dad would always have really good advice and we would have little talks about my daughter. I was always surprised at his wisdom, because I didn't think that he had that in him. Because when I was growing up, back in the fifties or the late forties, there weren't that many things that kids and teenagers did that got your parents all riled up. Back then, there were no drugs, no big sex parties. Not only have times changed, but my daughter was a bit of a rebel. He would talk to her. I don't know if it did any good, but it meant a lot to me that he at least tried."

"The nice thing about being a granddad is that you can spoil those grandchildren rotten, then take 'em home," said one granddad. Some even take this further and provide a fatherly influence, in this day and age of single-parent families. These granddads should be highly commended for their loving acts. When we daughters become mothers, we continue our journey with a new sense of father . . . grandfather.

A Chip Off the Ol' Block

A man finds out what is meant by a spitting image when he tried to feed cereal to his infant.

— IMOGENE FEY

Like father like daughter? Yes, that is often the case. Sometimes this turns out to be a good thing, sometimes a bit of a challenge. But most of us can find at least a part of ourselves that reminds us of our dads.

Carmen readily admits that she has many characteristics in common with her father. She said, "I was recently confronted with a similarity I have with my dad — the shape of our heads! While I was traveling, a gold crown from a back molar came loose. I went to the dentist once I returned and was told the reason it fell off was that I had bitten a hole clean through the gold cap. I immediately thought, 'Well, thanks, Dad!'

"That might seem odd, but I inherited my square jaw from my dad. Now that's fine with me, except for the fact that, because of this particular shape, when we bite down, we can generate a tremendous amount of pressure, more so than people with oval or heart-shaped faces. The down side is that both my dad and I crack our teeth in half, just by chewing. Both my dad and I have never had cavities. Our teeth are strong, but not strong enough to withstand the pressure of our jaws.

"I'm also a lot like my dad in more ways than just the physical. Our brains work a lot alike. We're both determined, more confident that we are right than we probably deserve to be, and we both love animals and, independently of each other, have decided to become vegetarians because we don't like the idea of hurting animals unnecessarily. We may have strong jaws, but we have soft hearts."

Fathers also recognize that special link with their daughters. Herman "Tex" Moton, an African-American, described his unique connection to his daughter, Nancy: "It's hard for me to talk about Nancy and not become emotional, because Nancy is named for my mother and her mother. I see so much of both of them in her, as it relates to determination and being positive about what she thinks and her will to live; you can't stop her. When I say a determined woman, I don't use that word lightly. She is not deterred by what someone says. She holds her convictions strongly, and she can see dishonesty a mile away. Nancy has an innate awareness of right and wrong. She'll say, 'Just because fifty-one percent of the people say it's right doesn't make it right.' If in her heart she's right, then she stays with it, and she has been encouraged by both her mother and myself to be that way.

" 'Feel it in here,' I tell her, 'and don't be affected by what you and I say, or her mother says, feel it in here,' he told us, patting his chest.

"Even though we think of parents influencing children more than the other way around, I believe she has given me the living proof that my mother still lives. I see the qualities which I experienced in my mother in Nancy, even though she barely got to know my mother before she died. My mother died not long after Nancy was born. I think and have always felt that the black woman is the greatest human on earth. I was raised by two, my grandmother and my mother. And my Nancy is just like them. I'm proud of her."

Not all father-daughter bonds require blood ties, however, as Toby, adoptive father of Christy, can attest. Christy was five years old when her mother married Toby. She was adopted by Toby when she was seven. He told us, "Christy is very, very quick-witted and outgoing. She has so much stamina. She sings at her college, she's been to the Republican National Convention, she's been on tours to Russia, she's been on tours to D.C. She's really a smart kid and definitely an overachiever.

"I would like to think that, because I became her father, I've introduced her to things that she would not have been able to experience. I feel I've brought stability to her situation. I hope that I was a very good father, that I was always there for her. She has suffered at times in her life from anorexia, but she's on top of that now and goes around speaking on the subject.

"Christy and I have done a lot of things together. The first time I was sworn in as a representative from the state of Texas she was there. She thought that was really special. Christy has been very, very supportive of me in a political position. She will debate you to death. Christy will take an opposite position, even though she doesn't believe in that position. She wants to be an attorney, and she's sharp enough, not just to be an attorney, but to be an exceptional attorney, like me!"

There's no lack of pride when it comes to a father being glad his daughter takes on his characteristics. We daughters are not too shy, either, when there's something we like about ourselves that we inherited from our fathers. It's good to take the moment, whether it's a good relationship or not, to observe how we became who we are and who helped us get here.

I Knew I Could Always
Count on Him

No one knows the true worth of a man but his family. The dreary man drowsing, drop-jawed, in the commuter train, the office bore, the taciturn associate — may be the pivot of a family's life, welcomed with hugs, told the day's news, asked for advice. No longer Mr. B, but Dad. No longer a nonentity but a man possessed of skills and wisdom; courageous and capable, patient and kind. Respected and loved.

— PAM BROWN

Wouldn't it be nice if life was a smooth journey comprised solely of successes, perfect health, and unconditional love? Well, no one we know has experienced this ideal. We've all had our share of defeats, disappointments, and rejection. At times like these, the truly fortunate daughters can turn to their dads for support.

Delores needed all the support she could get when, at age thirty-one, she was diagnosed with cancer. She recalled, "Just about everyone let me down. My mother fell apart and wasn't really a help at all. I couldn't count on my husband or friends. Everyone was so afraid back then, 'Oh, cancer. Oh my God.' They didn't know what to do, so they did nothing, which was worse than maybe doing something, even if it was wrong. My dad, however, was really helpful, just by being there for me. He didn't fall apart like everyone else. I needed someone to be strong. I knew I could count on him if I needed him for something, and he didn't fail me."

In the middle of a crisis, we all need extra support and the opportunity to draw on the strength of others. Prior to her divorce, Loraine had seen herself as a "stable person. But when I was going through my divorce, my ex-husband was really causing me a lot of grief. I had three kids, and my ex-husband was fighting me for custody. Then I got fired from my job, through all of this. So here I was unemployed, having just moved into an apartment with three kids. I thought I would lose my mind.

"I was an emotional basket case going through all of this. Finally it got to the point that I was so depressed, I checked myself into the hospital. My ex-husband called my father and told him, 'You need to have her committed. You need to do this!' And my father told my ex to get lost. He said, 'You're the one making her crazy, and leave her alone!'

"Then my dad immediately flew down from New York to be with us. Having him here made all the difference in the world. I know that anytime I ever call my dad and say, 'Dad, I need you now,' he will be there."

He Taught Me Everything
I Know About . . .

Did you know that Napoleon instituted the château system for French wines? I remember the difference between acceleration and velocity. I even know why airplanes fly. My head is full of information picked up from my dad. We used to talk at the dinner table about how things work.

— KAREN, VINCENT'S DAUGHTER

Our fathers can be a treasure chest of information, giving important skills and snippets of trivia we would rarely receive from our mothers. Lessons on how to hold a hammer, how to close a contract, how to stand your ground with a car mechanic — lessons that help us develop the confidence and competence needed to manage when we're out in the world on our own. Take one of the coauthors' fond remembrances of how she learned her sales techniques: "My daddy is the greatest salesman of all time. I know, for sure, he can get the best deal for a car that can be gotten. I remember when I had just moved to Nashville. I had gotten this great job. In fact, I landed the first management position for a woman in my field. I was getting a great deal of money for 1979. I was getting forty thousand dollars a year. In that town at that time, it was unheard of for a woman to be paid that much. My dad was so proud of me. He drove to Nashville from Odessa, Texas, to congratulate me . . . and to help me buy my first car. Yep, he was there to show me how it was done. One easy course on 'how to sell the salesman on what you want to spend for a car.' He was a wonderful professor of sales wit and wisdom that day. He was like an athlete of sales. It was so meaningful to me that only recently did I let that car go.

"If I have learned anything about selling, and my friends tell me that I could sell air to pilots, it is there's an art to selling. I learned the best of that art from my dad."

"When I was a little girl in the third grade I remember finding out the four points of selling:

1. The customer needs a product.
2. You have a product to sell.
3. You show that customer how he needs *your* product.
4. Close the deal.

"The most important thing about those four points is the final, fourth point. That's what daddy said. He felt that ninety-five percent of the mediocre salesmen in the whole world did not close that deal. Daddy talked that way, too. He sold me on selling the 'whole' world. Also, a great salesman always would work a 'good for you, good for me' deal. (He taught me win-win before that was popular.)"

Many times we don't even know we have abilities our fathers taught us until we have to use them. Take, for example, Marlice, who had moved away from home as a young, single woman, and was excited about purchasing her first car. She told us, "I was so proud of my Pontiac Sunbird. It was white on the outside with white interior, so it was a hard car to keep clean.

"A friend asked me to house-sit and I jumped at the chance because, unlike the apartment where I was living, there was space to wash my car. I washed and waxed the car inside my friends' spacious garage the night before. I waxed so hard that I developed painful tendonitis in my arms. It was worth it because the car sparkled. The next morning, I hopped into the car. Before I started the car I took a deep, long breath of the sweet smell of clean shiny white interior. Proud of my hard work, I started the car and put it into reverse. Something caught my eye on the right side of the car interior, and I turned my head as I drove the car out of the garage. Then I heard a loud crunch.

"While I was admiring my newly polished car, I'd forgotten to close the door before I started driving out of the garage. The car door crumpled in half as it hit the middle pole separating the car ports in the garage.

"Frantically, I stopped the car, got out, went into the house, and called my dad in Texas. He was calm and logical, methodically asking me questions, and then told me he'd call me back. A little while later he called, telling me he had called the Pontiac dealer I had purchased the car from in Texas, and then a body shop in Tennessee, and a tow truck was on the way. I learned that day the importance of staying calm and taking care of business."

This life lesson served Marlice in many situations later on. But none more important, perhaps, than the challenge she faced when her father was terminally ill with cancer, and the family was having a very hard time with all the emotional and emergency medical decisions. In the middle of the distress and turmoil, it was Marlice who was calm and cool, methodically asking questions of the doctors and nurses. It was because of the clear-headedness in crisis that she learned from her father that he lived his last days in comfort rather than in pain.

Just as Marlice used her skill in some of the crises of life, another may use skills learned from dads in everyday situations. Candice, a thirty-something single parent, told us that she relies on "maintenance" skills she learned from her father to take care of the little things that need fixing around her home. She told us, "My father never made me feel like I couldn't do something simply because I was a girl. In fact, he taught me things I suspect most dads teach their sons but never think to show their daughters.

"When I was around six, we made a go-cart together. We made it out of old crates; we sawed the wood, nailed it together, put wheels on it, and put in a steering rope, even a brake. I thought I was so cool! Not only was I the only kid on my block with a go-cart, I was definitely the only girl with a dad like mine. At the time, I was just having fun, but looking back on it, I realize that I learned how to measure and cut wood, the proper way to hold a hammer, how to figure out basic mechanical functions, and which way to screw in a screw. Now, as a single parent with not a lot of extra cash, being able to diagnose and fix things around the house, to hang curtain rods and keep things up without paying a repairman, means a lot to me. I don't know if he knew at the time how much that go-cart meant to me, but certainly now I treasure the experience all the more."

Candice's story is not unique in that many of the women we interviewed told us how simple childhood experiences that might have seemed unimportant or common at the time dramatically shaped their lives as adult women. An accomplished author told us that she learned her craft of storytelling by listening to the stories her father used to tell her when she was a little girl. She told us, "My dad was such a great storyteller. We'd be at dinner, or driving in the car, and he'd tell us about some adventure he'd had the day before. I remember sitting in rapt attention, convinced that he was the bravest, strongest, most exciting man that had ever been born. He could make the simplest story sound magical."

With sadness in her voice, she said, "He now is in the last stages of Alzheimer's disease, and even when he mumbles away in incoherent ramblings, there's a storylike rhythm. He called me with the speed-dial recently. I don't think he really knew who he was calling. It is as if he's still trying to tell me another great story, about the adventures he's having . . . and somewhere in my heart I believe him."

Sometimes we don't even realize how much our fathers have influenced our ways of making business decisions. Marlice told us, "I watched how my dad conducted his business affairs. One time all of his friends were going in on a particular investment and he decided to pass. I asked him why, especially since it seemed like such a great opportunity and all his friends were going for it. He wasn't a man of many words. He looked at me and said simply, 'If a deal sounds too good to be true, it usually is.' Sure enough, the deal went sour and all his friends lost their shirts.

"Now, before I make any investment, I meticulously check out all aspects of the deal before I make a decision. People even say that I remind them of my father, because I have a healthy cynicism about opportunities. I like being compared with him.

Whether it's selling, staying calm in a crisis, tightening the screws on the kitchen cabinets, or being conscious of a good deal, dads can have profound and long-term effects on the way we approach important aspects of our lives. Not only do we learn the skills themselves, but more importantly, our fathers teach us that *we can* — we can take care of ourselves, and we can rely on our fathers and other trustworthy men when we need to ask for help. A sense of competency is a valuable lesson that many loving fathers pass on to their daughters.

He Taught Me to Care

The words that a father speaks to his children in the privacy of home are not heard by the world, but as in whispering-galleries, they are clearly heard at the end and by posterity.

— JEAN PAUL RICHTER

I've learned that you shouldn't go through life with a catcher's mitt on both hands. You need to be able to throw something back.

— ANONYMOUS

Often without knowing it, we take on characteristics like those of our fathers. This is especially significant when women learn how to care for and about others by watching their fathers actively helping those in need.

Rita shared, "My father was a very generous man and he helped a lot of people. Friends who were down-and-out, he'd take in and let them stay at our home, cousins, family members. He was just very kindhearted. He would get in trouble because there are so many homeless, but he would never go by someone without giving them money. We weren't rich, by any means, but he was a very generous man. And I think that's what he left behind, because I hear it about me.

"More than anything, my dad has taught me to enjoy life to its fullest every single day. He has taught me that worrying is pointless, because only God knows what tomorrow will hold. His easy, laid-back demeanor is something for which I will always strive. I always know that if he is truly angry over something, it's worth being angry over. All my life I heard of kids growing up with fathers who were unpredictable. They never knew if dad would come home angry or happy. They were almost afraid of their dads. I've never had to wonder or be afraid of my dad coming home. I always knew he'd walk in the door thrilled to see me and my mom. I knew that no matter what happened at work that day, he left it at work. Home time was family time."

Fathers not only teach their daughters how to care about those outside the family, but about those in the family as well. Mary Lynn told us how her dad's caring affected her: "He dropped out of the eighth grade to work. His family was very poor and he always worked hard to make us a living. He had a cotton gin and two blackland farms. I stayed with Grandma in Roanoke, Texas and went to high school there the last couple of years. I graduated from high school when I was seventeen. There were only three graduates that year, 1929. All eleven grades were in the same school. It was a very hard time, but his foremost thought was for us all to get an education, because he didn't have one. He cared so much that during the week I stayed there in Roanoke with my grandma and he'd come and pick me up and take me home on the weekends. Commuting in those days was unheard of, but my dad was committed that I would have a high school degree.

"Since education was so important to my dad, I tried

to stress it to all three of my children. I am eighty-six, and my oldest son, who is fifty-three, went back to college, and as of this year, all three of my children have bachelor's degrees."

Another adult daughter speaks proudly of her dad. Gloria said, "I also admire the fact that my dad has always been so supportive of my mom. She's been in a very high-profile career. He could have allowed this to be threatening to him. Instead, he supported her and the ministry she's so involved in. Not every man is secure enough to do this. My dad was very religious, more religious than my mother was, I think. As far as today, my husband, Toby, is very religious. He knows an awful lot about the Bible. And I see the same characteristics in my father as I see in Toby. So, I guess I married someone who had some of dad's characteristics. I think my father worked very hard for his family, and he cared a lot about his family, and he loved his family.

"My dad had a kind of a short temper, and I know I have that, but I also care. My father taught me how to be a very caring person. One of the characteristics that my daughter has said about me is, 'If you made a friend with my mother, she'll be a friend of yours forever,' and I think that's what my father has taught me. Just to reach out to others and know I've made a difference makes me realize that even though my dad has been gone for sixteen years, he's still touching lives through me."

Caring is an art passed down from generation to generation, just as cruelty and family dysfunction can plague a family for years to come. When our fathers teach us the joys of giving to others, they not only touch our lives in a powerful way, but also the lives of all the people that we, in turn, love. Even though many of the people we help will never meet our fathers, they nevertheless experience the impact of the caring way our dads lived their lives.

My Daughter, My Teacher

You can learn many things from children.
How much patience you have, for instance.

— FRANKLIN P. JONES

We daughters learn a lot from our dads — but the reverse is also true. They learn a great deal about life and themselves as our fathers. The dads we talked to gushed with stories about how much they admired, as well as learned from, their little girls.

Perhaps one of the first things dads learn from us is the lesson of self-love. Michael expressed his gratitude for how becoming a parent has helped shape and refine his character. He said, "I was a very selfish person before we had children. We went to movies whenever we wanted to, just picking up, doing stuff, taking off whenever we wanted. But once we had Megan, our lives revolved around this little being in our lives, this little gift from God. Our needs came second. So, my daughter taught me how to be selfless. Taught me how to love — it's a brand-new kind of love. I have a totally different kind of love for my wife than I do for my parents. When you have your own child, you realize it's all centered around God's love. How could you not love a child that you had a small part in creating?"

A daughter can provide a reference point for a father — help ground him and help him sort out what's really important. In a day and age when external accomplishment and career advancement are so highly prized, loving a daughter can help bring a dad back to basics. David, a graduate student, told us, "I've got a lot of friends who are married and reluctant to have children because of the time raising children takes away from studying. I'm so glad we had Alexandra, because she's been my sanity. It's insane to give your life completely, utterly to a graduate program. It's really out of balance. Alexandra has given me balance.

"It's one thing being married. There's a level of negotiation that one has to carry on with that kind of commitment. With a child, you can't negotiate, at least I can't. I can't say, 'Tough. This much time is mine.' I have to be here for my daughter, and I have to give my wife a break so she can have some time to herself. Having a child has forced me into a slower rhythm of life. I'm really grateful for that."

Slowing down and assessing priorities can affect some of a man's most important life decisions, and give him hope for positive change. Vito told us, "I believe that if it wasn't for my daughters' love drawing me back to home, I wouldn't have lasted this long in our marriage. We have had some problems, but thank God, we are doing well now. I came from a family that was very dysfunctional. I know now that I can change that and I want to model a good family for my daughters."

In addition to serving as a point of reference, daughters can teach their dads important lessons simply by being themselves. Gary told us that his daughter, Carrie

Ann, had taught him "that it is important to know who you are. At an early age my daughter had a real strong sense of who she is. It doesn't mean that she handles everything perfectly or anything, but I feel like through it all she always keeps aware of who she is. She knows what she likes. She knows what she doesn't like. Of course, as adults we have to learn how to kind of go with the flow because you don't get what you want. That's part of the maturing process. But as a young lady I think she has a really strong sense of who she is, and I think that's important. Watching her has encouraged me to take an honest look at myself and see who I am and see how God's wired me. I think it's important to know who you are."

John, father of four girls, has learned different lessons from different daughters. John is an outgoing, extroverted, fun-loving man who enjoys conversation. He told us how his twin daughters, Abigail and Amanda, have taught him that it's okay just to be quiet. He said, "If you get my older daughters, Tiffani and Melissa, together, they just talk up a storm. Abigail and Amanda, however, can sit in the car with their hands folded and they're just quiet. At first it bothered me, because I didn't know what they were thinking. It's taken me forever to learn that they're not being uncooperative or uncommunicative. They still love me and they aren't mad at me. Everything is all right in the world and it's okay to be quiet. I've never been around anybody like that. I've learned from them that not everyone is extroverted, nor does everyone like to talk all the time, or say everything that's on top of their mind."

Being able to see things from a daughter's point of view can expand a father's perspective. Sometimes realizing that this little girl is looking to her father to be good, strong, and kind can be just the inspiration some men need to "turn over a new leaf," as Michael told us: "I decided I was going to be a nicer guy. I would always be a little more, I don't want to say honest, because I don't want you to think that I outright lied. But I was once a car salesman. While I never lied to sell the cars, I never told the whole truth either.

"Watching my daughter deal with having brain cancer right after she was born has turned my life upside down, and actually helped me put my priorities in the right order. Before Misha was born, I had never really been a religious man. I always believed in God, but I realized that I needed to take my spirituality more seriously, because I was changing somehow by helping my daughter. I needed to realize that there is hope, and that God can help me keep going.

"I remember we had taken her back to the doctor's when Misha was one and a half years old and she hadn't learned how to walk yet. She was still crawling. The physical therapist said, 'Well, Misha's surprising us. We expected her to be in diapers until she's five, she's actually crawling now, so maybe she'll start walking when she's two and a half or three.' Everyone was projecting so negatively, and I thought, 'You're just the biggest bunch of idiots I have ever seen in my entire life. The only reason I come here is that I don't know how to operate, or I would do it myself.'

"I left fighting a sense of discouragement. I had been looking for work, and because I had decided to be honest, I didn't lie on my résumé or tell perspective employers that I was working when I wasn't. When they asked me why I wasn't working, I would tell them that my daughter was sick. Because of that honesty, every job I was offered was taken away. It seemed that people didn't want to have someone who had a sick daughter. Well, I decided to stick by the truth. If I lost jobs, then that's the way it would be.

"The day before my birthday, back in 1994, I had an interview at a company, and right then and there they offered me the job. Then one of the interviewers looked closer at my résumé and asked me, 'What was the reason that you didn't work at this time?' And I told him. The guy retracted the offer and said, 'We'll call you tomorrow and let you know if you have the job.' I knew I'd never hear from them, and I didn't.

"I left feeling discouraged. So I drove home, thinking it's been a bad day. But then I reminded myself, 'It's not a bad day, because to me a bad day is when they tell you your daughter's going to die.' When that happens, you realize what's really a bad day.

"When I got home, Misha was hanging onto the couch. She has right-side body weakness because she was totally paralyzed on the right side of her face. She smiled at me, looking like Popeye, and I thought, something's going on. I said, 'Hi Misha, come to Daddy.' And she walked! I just stood there, and she walked and walked. And it wasn't even a walk, by most people's standards. She walked straight to the T.V. and pointed at something on the T.V., and she wanted it to happen, and she just walked for me.

"That affected me. Even though at times it's still hard for me to see hope for myself, I have hope for my daughter. I want to live up to the values I believe in, no matter what happens, with the same tenacity that Misha has. She's tenacious, she doesn't give up on anything. I learned a long time ago that I was never the strongest, I was never the biggest, I wasn't really ever the best. So, if the first race came along and I lost, I realized I can win later on; if I was a good sprinter, I could figure a way to win in the end. It was always what you did tomorrow that mattered, long-term. The doctors could put a label on Misha, but she would never quit. She would bypass all of their predictions. And so would I."

As Michael and Misha demonstrate, the courage, integrity, and tenacity fathers see in their daughters can inspire them to go beyond the limits they had previously dared to challenge. Misha isn't the only daughter who has inspired her father to keep going and expect more out of himself. Martin told us how his daughter's commitment to her dream challenged him to make a major change in his own life. Martin had lived a rough life, shaped in large part by time served in Vietnam. He recalled, "I went over to Vietnam, running around in the jungle, killing people, and doing all kinds of things. When I came back, I went into law enforcement and ended up working on the streets of L.A. and dealing with the gangs and really experiencing life in that atmosphere, real, true life that goes on out there. I was a probation officer in L.A. County, and I must have raised probably thousands of kids over ten years, and reeducated parents on how to raise their kids. I was more a parent educator than a child-rehab counselor."

Martin's story takes a unique turn in that he didn't get to know his daughter until she was a teenager, having given her up for adoption when she was born: "When I met my daughter, I was working as a disciplinarian in a big school district. She had been raised by a guy who had built custom homes and grew up with a silver spoon in her mouth, until she was fourteen. When he died, the family kind of fell apart, and she started getting involved with alcohol and boys. I thought I pretty well knew what my daughter was about after about a year, until one day she called me and said, 'I've been doing crack for two years, and you had no idea. I'm in a halfway house because I almost died last night from an overdose.'

"All of a sudden, the tables have turned. Now I'm the parent experiencing what other parents have been going through. It's a lot different when you're counseling than when you're the parent with kids on drugs and placing them in rehab settings. That really opened my eyes.

"She got out of the halfway house and began working

as a secretary. One day she called and said, 'You know, you've been telling me I need a career and I need to go back to school. I've finally decided what I want to be.' I thought, 'Great she's going to pick a career.' And she said, 'I'm going to be an actress. I'm going to be a movie star.' I thought, 'Okay, I'd better work a little harder with her and bring her to reality.'

"Fortunately, I didn't succeed. She went to school to study acting and then changed her focus to directing and producing. When she finished up her film courses at Orange Coast, she invited me and my wife to attend awards night. They showed all of the top entries that had won awards, which included hers. The other entries were all these romance stories while hers was of street hookers and drug addicts and what was going on in the real world. That really impressed me. She experienced what the real world was about, and I think she'll probably succeed. She has a lot of compassion for people who are addicted to different things, and I know she'll make some pretty good films.

"I learned from her that you can be anything you want to be. You have to follow your heart. So, I decided to make changes in my own life. I always wanted to be a doctor, so in '92 I quit my counseling job for the state and I went into pre-med. I'm doing my internship right now. I owe my inspiration to my daughter, that I could even aspire to this, much less actually do it. Enough said."

Section Four

Troubles and Triumphs

There are times when parenthood seems nothing but feeding the hand that bites you.

— PETER DE VRIES

Why Did He Leave Us?

*Well, being divorced is like being hit with a Mack truck.
If you live through it, you start looking very carefully
to the right and to the left.*

— JEAN KERR

Divorce rips families apart and breaks the hearts of the children torn between their parents. Regardless of what has occurred "behind closed doors," often one parent is seen as the "bad guy" for leaving or initiating the divorce. Such was Elizabeth's experience when her parents divorced after thirty years of marriage. She recalled, "I remember being so disappointed in my dad for leaving us. I insisted on going to court the day the divorce was declared final. My mom didn't want to take me, but I was mad about the whole situation and I wanted to be there. She told me it was something she wanted to do by herself. I didn't believe that and, already being really angry about the situation, made my own decision that I was going to be there to support her. I was of driving age already, so when she left to go to court that day, I did, too. I just went by a different route. I got there ahead of her and I remember seeing her walk into the court building. She was a determined woman that day.

"That determination melted into tears when she saw that I had beaten her there. Honestly, I got my determination from both my parents. She then wouldn't let me go into the courtroom. She felt that it would scar me emotionally. However, when you are seventeen years old, you think your parents really do not know what's going on with the world, and you, of course, have *all* the insight that has been created since the beginning of the universe.

"She was right and I was wrong. I waited outside in the hall, sitting on a light oak bench. I had looked at every etching on that old bench. I suppose many people had been sitting there waiting for some horrible judgment to befall them or their family. So, I made a value judgment on the spur of the moment, again. After all, it worked the first time. I got up and quietly tiptoed over to the two huge cherry-wood doors that separated me from those hallowed chambers.

"When I opened those doors, I got the shock of my life. There was my mother sitting next to her attorney. Then there was another attorney, but my father was not there. There were only a couple of other people in the room, but my daddy that I loved so much was not one of them. I closed those doors and just stood there in a world of my own. My dad did not have the courage to face my mom in court. My dad, strong as a bull, was at that moment a coward, a chicken, a jerk, and a big wienie! He had sent his attorney to do his dirty work. In that moment, I felt lied to, cheated, and, most of all, disappointed. That day changed me forever. Just like my mom had predicted, it had scarred me. It took years to get over the disappointment she had tried to spare me, and my dad and I paid a very heavy price for my decision."

Traditionally, divorce means the loss of daily contact

with one's father. When Thomas and his first wife were divorced, he initially retained custody of his son and daughter. He and his daughter, Linnell, were practically inseparable. He told us, "Linnell was a tomboy. I couldn't do anything that Linnell wouldn't come along. I couldn't work in the yard, that Linnell wasn't there. I couldn't go to the grocery store, that Linnell didn't want to go. Whenever you saw me, you'd see Linnell.

"Then Linnell went to move to her mom's and it was a bad situation. And it shouldn't have happened, but it did. It was problematic then, and it still is. Linnell lived with her mom for about three years, from the time she was about thirteen until she was about sixteen and after she got out of high school. After that, she got a job, and went to college. Even though she lived with her mom, Linnell's always known that I would take care of everything. She always came to me for everything, and it's still that way. But the divorce has definitely affected her. She lost the stability in her life that she needed. If I could give her anything, I'd give her back her childhood."

Like Thomas, other divorced fathers told us how hard it was for them to be separated from their children. Allen lives in San Diego and his daughter, Linda, is in Phoenix with her mother. He said, "It's painful because my daughter and I are very good friends. In fact, she considers me her best friend right now. We talk on the phone around two hours each week. Very often she calls me when she needs encouragement.

"When I do get to see her, we sit on the couch together

and she hugs me. After a few minutes, she'll flip her shoes off and she'll say, 'Daddy, can you rub my feet.' That's very typical of how we connect. We can sit and talk for hours while I sit there and rub her feet. I pity her husband, because I know he's gonna have to do that!

"On a day-to-day basis, though, it is so difficult not to be able to tuck her into bed or comb her hair, make up a story with funny voices, and pray the way we used to. It consoles her and me, too! Even now, when she's at my house she'll ask for the Cinderella story that I created with these special characters. The difficulty is not being there. Just the physical presence of being there."

The pain in a father's heart who misses his daughter can be matched only by the pain in the heart of the little girl who needs her daddy. Such is the story of Princess Pale Moon, an American Indian woman, who shared the pain she suffered when she lost contact with her father when she was seven. She told us, "One night I heard my momma and daddy arguing, so I hid under the table in the kitchen. There was only a bedroom and a kitchen in this shack located near the Indian reservation. I heard my mom say, 'Get out of this house and don't ever come back. I don't ever want to see your face again.' I thought, 'Please, please, Daddy don't go, don't go.' Then I cringed as I heard the door slam. I knew that was it. My mom went back into the bedroom and slammed the door. I slipped out from underneath the table and tiptoed over to the door, hoping I could beg my daddy not to leave us. It was dark and I listened to see if he was there, but he wasn't. He was gone. I just sat in the dark and cried.

"Very shortly after that, my mom took me and my brother and sister to an orphanage. We were there for two years. I remember children rocking back and forth mumbling to themselves; some were banging their heads on the wall. I remember loud music and a heavyset lady who had teeth missing. She must have been in charge, because once she dragged me down the hall by my long black Indian hair. For those two years, my hair was never cut. I felt so unloved. I cried for my daddy to come and take me away. I felt close to him because I look more like him, more Indian, than my siblings.

"One day Mom came back and took us to a second orphanage. The lady there made us memorize Bible verses. We had chores to do, like milk goats and bring them in. We couldn't have dinner unless we had those verses memorized. My brother and I started singing in church. We sang 'Love Lifted Me.' He stood on a chair beside me on stage.

"That was my hope, that someone would love us and take us away. In my heart of hearts, I wanted that to be my daddy. I still thought all the time about my daddy. I wondered why I hadn't received a letter from him, as I thought we were so close. I didn't realize that my mother kept him from us.

"Finally Mom came back for us and took us to Tennessee, where we lived in a two-room apartment. I kept asking her, was Daddy going to come and see us. All eight of his brothers and sisters lived in the same town. My father's parents were the only grandparents I had. But I was not allowed to ever visit them. She always told me that Dad didn't want to come and see us. She never told us that she told him he can never see us. I have since gone back and found the divorce papers and she did have full custody. My dad didn't have visitation rights.

"My mom always sent me to the courthouse to pick up the child support check. This was so traumatic for me. I would beg her not to have to do it. I think she was afraid she might run into him, so she sent me. He supported us until we were eighteen. There were three times when the check lapsed, and he went to jail. I went back to that courthouse as a forty-year-old adult to face that fear of how I felt. While I was there I got his death certificate, their marriage certificate, and the divorce papers.

"In junior high school, my main sense of loss was there was only one person to make decisions about me. There was only one person to believe me or not, give me information about life. All three of us were really good kids. We didn't get in trouble or give my mom cause to worry. Still, we couldn't have any friends over. Not once in my life did I get to have a slumber party or have one friend over. I imagined if Daddy was there, he would say, 'I think it's okay for her to go to the football game or to the party. Or, 'Why don't you let her friend come over and spend the night. She'll be okay, trust her.' I was never trusted. Mother's decision came out of being neglected herself. Later, we found out she was mentally ill, and that was part of the illness, being paranoid. I have learned to forgive and love my mom today. She did the best she could with what she had to work with in her life.

"I vowed that someday I would find my dad. My sister, brother, and I continued to sing together after we left the orphanage. Once we performed at the Civic Auditorium. My brother was a hit, standing on the chair, belting this high voice between me and my sister. I went upstairs later to watch the rest of the show. As we were coming down the stairs into the lobby, we looked out into the crowd and I saw my daddy. He'd probably seen the advertisement and had come to see what we look like. He looked right at me and our eyes locked for a split second. Before I could smile and wave at him to come, he turned and was gone in the crowd. It was huge and I kept trying to find him.

"I told my mom because I was so excited. She said, 'Don't you ever, ever talk to him!' So, I knew I couldn't tell her how much I loved him and thought he was so handsome. So, I vowed even greater that someday I would find him. I knew it would have to be after I left home.

"Years later, I was married with three little boys. I decided it was time to go back to find Daddy. I went back to where we had lived and looked in the phone directory to see if I could find my daddy or his parents' name. They were not listed. I found my aunt's number and drove to her house from the directory address. I was scared to death to meet her. I was so afraid that she would say, 'I don't ever want to talk to you because of what your mom did to my brother.' But when she opened the door she said, 'You are John's daughter!' We hugged and hugged. Those hugs healed a lot of hurt.

"Right away, she started calling my dad's relatives to come over and see me. It was a reunion, a full house of cousins, aunts, and uncles that I had never met before. It was exciting! One of my half-sisters pulled me aside and said, 'Let me tell you about your daddy. Your daddy really loved you, no matter what you thought or what you heard. But your daddy is gone.' I said, 'What, he moved away.' She said, 'No, he passed away.' I said, 'Oh, oh, I am too late.' She started to comfort me, that I had found them. She told me that just two weeks before he died he sat where I was sitting and cried and said, 'I never got to see my kids grow up. I wonder how my little girls and son are doing.' He laid his head down on his arms and cried.

"When I went to the cemetery to find his grave, I found that his remains had been moved by his second wife. Just last year, I finally tracked down where she had lived. But I was afraid she would reject me, so I put it off. Nine months later, I finally wrote her and sent her a picture of me and my family. Right away, I got a letter from her daughter saying that her mom had passed away. I was so sad to be late again. Her reply—'You look just like Daddy'—reminded me that, after all, my daddy was her daddy, too. So, soon I will be on my way to see her and her sister to find out more about the daddy I desperately loved and never got to know."

Divorce is defined in Webster's dictionary as "total separation." As these stories illustrate, however, the hearts bonded between father and daughter can never be totally torn asunder.

We Didn't See Him Much

Where you used to be, there is a hole in the world,
which I find myself constantly walking around in the daytime,
and falling into at night.

— EDNA ST. VINCENT MILLAY

Divorce isn't the only reason daughters are separated from their dads. Gloria told us about seeing her dad only on the weekends because he "worked for the Santa Fe Railroad and he came home on the weekends only. My brothers and sister and I used to run down to the end of Farmer Market Road and wait for him to come home on Friday nights. We waited and waited and waited.

"My mother always tried to make his homecoming on Friday night eventful for him, 'cause he worked all week. She'd say, 'Now, we're going to have homemade ice cream,' we had the crank and everything. 'Now, don't tell Daddy.' So, the first thing I'd do when I saw him: 'Daddy, guess what we're having, homemade ice cream.' It's too hard to keep a secret when you're a little girl, and you haven't seen him all week long.

"I still remember how we used to sit at the table at dinnertime. I sat next to my father. At the time, I didn't think much about that, but when I look back on it now, getting to sit by him means a lot to me. We used to sit around and link hands and say prayers at the dinner table, just like in *The Waltons*. We did that before *The Waltons'* show ever took place. My father sat at the end of the table, and then it was me, my sister, and my mother on the end and my two brothers on the other side of the table.

"I can also remember, on Sunday afternoons, we went with my dad to work in the field. We were Seventh-Day Adventists, and we went to church on Saturday, so on Sunday afternoon, we went out, and my dad worked, always worked. My dad was a very hard worker.

Some dads have to leave their families due to work obligations. Others leave to serve their country. Muriel recalled meeting her dad after he had served in Vietnam. She said, "My father left when I was five years old and was gone for one and a half years of my life when he was in Vietnam. We would send him audiotapes weekly. It was quite the ritual sitting at the kitchen counter with Mommy prompting me to relay the happenings of my world, while the next brother to talk stared blandly and played with paper clips until I was done. Though having distinct memories of my father prior to his VN stint, during that time I forgot who he was — and associated only the concept of far away and the sound of his voice on the tapes he would send back to us with 'Daddy.' Every night at the end of my prayer, I would say, 'and God bless Daddy and all the soldiers in Vietnam and may they come home soon, safe and sound.'

"When my father did come home it was an exciting day for us all. We drove a long way to Travis AFB, a Navy base in northern California. There we were with thousands of other people having exciting days too. We waited for hours for all these army personnel to land and deplane. I watched all these children and women kissing their returning family members through the Cyclone fence as the men proceeded in a line to a final screening point. I wanted to kiss my dad through the Cyclone fence! I was so excited. It's all I could think about. 'Hurry up, Daddy. So I can kiss you through the fence!'

"I distinctly remember the panic I experienced as my brothers and mother all excitedly yelled, 'There he is!' when he exited the plane. And I, at age six, craned my neck and scanned the sea of uniformed men to locate my father. The terrifying reality for me was, I didn't know who I was looking for! What did he look like? Everyone else was so excited. I was excited because finally I had someone to kiss through the Cyclone fence — but which man on the other side was he? Who do I ask for a kiss? Somehow I finally matched his face with my memory — and I got a kiss through the fence. Our family was reunited."

Some reunions occur long after the daughter's childhood has ended, as in the case of the daughter placed for adoption. Both father and daughter are affected by the separation. Martin shared with us how his daughter was adopted: "When I was in college, my first true romance started. We went away for a week of camping and came back; eventually we broke up, but during that week she got pregnant. Back in the middle sixties, birth control was something they didn't tell you about.

"So, after about three months of not seeing her, she

showed up at my parents' house and told me in secret, 'I'm pregnant.' I was scared to death because her dad was a cop. She refused to tell him, but after six or seven months, it was pretty obvious. So her parents and my parents got involved and worked out a plan. I paid the hospital bills, while she went off to a girl's home and had the baby. I thought she was going to keep the baby. I heard that she had gotten married to some guy in the military, so I figured they were raising the baby together.

"I was drafted and went to Vietnam. The whole time I was in the service, I thought about her raising my daughter who I would never see again. Then I got injured in the service, and couldn't have children. My daughter was always in the back of my mind.

"Years went by. One summer I was living in Arizona and I was sitting around the pool at the apartment where I lived and started talking to a guy who also lived in the complex. He told me about how his daughter was given up for adoption and that she showed up, as an adult, at his front door. There was this gorgeous twenty-one-year-old knocking on his door, calling him 'Dad,' and he didn't know what to do. That started me thinking.

"At that time I was a probation officer and I'd worked with kids for about ten years with the county, and every girl that came through my office who had about the same birthday, I would look at her and wonder if she were my daughter. One day, about nineteen years after my daughter was born, my mother called and said, 'We got a call from your ex-girlfriend, and you probably didn't know that your daughter was put up for adoption. Your ex then married and had another child almost two years to the day that your daughter was born. Your daughter's looking for you and she wants to meet you.'

"So I found out she was also living in Arizona, and I got her phone number and we finally connected late that night. We made a date to meet. She was working in an office down in Fashion Island, so I took off at lunch and walked into this office and saw a couple of girls standing together talking. I realized that one of them was my daughter, but I couldn't tell which one. One of them smiled and said, 'It's me, Dad.' I was just amazed. I just kept looking at her, saying, 'You're my daughter!' I just couldn't believe it. I'm so glad that that happened, because I can't have any more kids.

"We went out and had lunch. I brought a stack of pictures of things that I had done since childhood and we talked and talked. She wanted to have dinner together, so she could show me her photos. I invited her to have dinner with me and my wife. She came over, and the very first picture in her album was of her and her boyfriend. My wife went upstairs and got a picture out of her album of that very same boy from her special education class, maybe five or six years prior. Amazing connections!

"It was good for both of us to meet and get to know each other. When she was five or six years old, her adoptive parents had written a letter to the agency asking for information about her birth parents. They wrote back and gave them the whole situation, so they went on to find out who we were and what we were doing. When she turned eighteen, my daughter decided to look us up. Her adoptive father had been killed in a car accident when she was thirteen, so having me in her life really filled a void in more ways than one. And she certainly filled a void in mine."

Many adopted children and their birth parents wonder about each other during the years of separation. Jessica, who was adopted as an infant, found her birth father after twenty-five years of "not knowing who my biological dad was. I loved my adoptive dad, but I was curious about my biological dad. From the first moment I met him, I was his flesh and blood."

However, the fantasy of finding one's biological father and the reality of building a realistic relationship can be at odds with each other. And it's not only the daughter's expectations that can be disappointed. Dads can also carry around a fantasy picture of his lost "little girl." Jessica told us that she and her birth father have had many struggles together. She said, "I have had to square off with him around his expectations of me. When I am not acting daughterly enough for him, he gets upset and communication stops. I have no idea what the problem is and have to absolutely drag it out of him, which sometimes takes days or even weeks. I basically told him I love you because of who you are in my life, but I don't need this. Then we sought professional advice, and found out ways to compromise. He will figure out what is bugging him, and every twenty-four hours will communicate with me to say, 'I am not ready to talk yet'. . . until he is. I've agreed not to blow up and to wait until he is finished processing."

Learning how to relate to each other without having years of history together may be challenging and demanding, but the effort can pay off. Jessica explained, "One day at the beach we were sitting on the sand, and the waves were rolling up. We were talking about my adoption, and he told me, 'I didn't feel like I had a purpose until you came back into my life. Now I know I have a reason to live.' That was a special moment I'll always treasure."

When a dad or daughter is physically absent, especially if that separation continues for months or even years, there is a longing for connection. When they finally get to spend time together, there is a special place in both hearts reserved for that unique bond between dad and daughter.

It Would Have Been Better If . . .

Words have an awesome impact. The impressions made by a father's voice can set in motion an entire trend of life.

— GORDON MACDONALD

The more fallible and more human and vulnerable he is, the more my respect for him has grown.

— CYNTHIA, HARRY'S DAUGHTER

We all wish our dads would live up to our fantasies. While no father is perfect, there are some dads, unfortunately, who, rather than be protective and kind, are abusive and cruel. A few women shared their difficult stories with us, about dads who fell far short of the ideal, who damaged, rather than protected, their daughters.

Patti, now in her thirties, told us about how, as a little girl, she would hide in the closet while her dad raged and yelled at her mother. She said, "I never remember him hitting her. But he would scream at Mom until she cried, broken, collapsed like a rag doll on the chair. I was so frightened and upset that I couldn't protect her. He didn't yell at me until I became a teenager, and then my mother and I both got it. I remember burying my head in my pillow on the nights he had his episodes, swearing I'd never marry a man like him. Never. No doubt that's one reason why I've never married.

"I lived in fear of him for years, long after I left the house. Eventually, I stood up to him with the help of a therapist. My dad was furious that I would tell anyone about what he called 'our private business.' He was so angry that he denied it ever happened. But I held my ground and told him if he wanted any contact with me, he'd have to comply with certain guidelines, such as always meeting in a public place, accepting the fact that I'd always bring someone with me, and that if there were any hint of a blowup, I'd simply walk away. I promised myself that I'd never get trapped by one of his rages again.

"Things have gone much better in the past six or seven years, now that I've set these boundaries. I've been surprised at how cooperative he's been. It makes me wonder if, on some level, he might feel guilty about the past and, without admitting it, is trying to make it up to me. I know underneath it all he loves me. However, sometimes his rage just gets the best of him and we've all suffered because of it."

We daughters are most vulnerable to abuse when we are young, when we are physically small and emotionally dependent. That is not to say we are immune to mistreatment once we have reached adulthood. Deena told us that "when I was in my early twenties, I moved to Philadelphia to sing in a dinner show. I didn't have any family close by. One time I got the flu. I was really sick and I called home, saying I really need someone to come and take care of me. I needed to come home and rest and have somebody wait on me. So my dad said he would drive up and get me and bring me home.

"You know the old saying, 'The show must go on?' Well, there were no understudies and the producers expected me to sing whether I was sick or not. Dad met me at the dinner theater, knowing I was going to have to get through the performance. I was up there with 104° fever waiting to get off stage, crawl into the car, and go to sleep. During the hour and a half that I was on stage, he proceeded to get snockered.

"When I realized my father was getting drunk, I called the producer over and asked for his help in trying to get the car keys away from my father. Dad hit me when I told him he was too drunk to drive. Finally, with the producer's help, he agreed to give me the keys, but as soon as we got in the car, he started berating me over the fact that I embarrassed him. 'How dare I take the keys away from him, and humiliate him in front of other people?' I remember praying that he would just fall asleep, pass out or something, so I could drive home in peace. I was exhausted, really sick, and very angry that here I was having to take care of him when he was supposed to be taking care of me. But instead of falling asleep, he screamed at me for two solid hours until we got home.

"When I hit the front door, I said to my mother, 'Your husband is drunk!' They had a big fight behind closed doors. I remember hearing my dad say, 'I'm not drunk.' My mom said, 'I hope you're drunk, because I'd hate to think you hit your own daughter when you were sober.' It was awful. He just denied it, and never did apologize to me.

"It has taken years of setting boundaries and standing up to my father, but our relationship has changed and healed in many ways. He's finally becoming the father I always wanted him to be. I have discovered my own personal power through this process. Now a 'dry' alcoholic, my father has softened and matured in his old age. I see a lot of regret and sorrow in him now. He's the one who says 'I love you' first. He says it with sincerity and warmth. Each time I hear it, I hear an 'I'm sorry. Let me make it better now' in there, too.

"Since Mom died a few months ago, he treats each encounter with me as if it may be our last. I can't ask for more than that. I finally feel safe with my dad; healing and forgiveness is replacing the hurt and anger. I'm one of the lucky ones. It looks like we get to have a 'happy ending' after all."

Ideally, daughters need to rely on their fathers to use their power to protect, not harm them. If dads misuse their strength, trying to dominate or intimidate their daughters, these women can go through life fearful and wary of men in general. Kimberly told us that she grew to fear her father's anger when she was a girl, and that now, as an adult, she has put her foot down. She said, "I think my relationship with my dad would have been better if I had been less afraid of him and learned earlier to communicate clearly about how things he does affect me. I have learned that when I want to state my feelings about something difficult, sending him a letter is more productive than talking, either in person or on the phone. I am not afraid of his anger anymore, and have more power in the relationship, because I now decide how close we will be, and what I will and won't do."

Kimberly's story illustrates a theme we heard time and again from women who had abusive fathers — misuse of power. To overcome the ill effects daughters must first regain personal power that their fathers have tried to keep from them. Then the challenge is to use that power positively. It is quite an undertaking, but many women we interviewed were clearly up to the task.

Sheena grew up having a love-hate relationship with her dad. Adoring him, on the one hand for his kindness and the special attention he gave her, and loathing the fact that he sexually abused her when she was four. Once an adult, and after years of secrecy, Sheena began seeing a therapist and told the truth about her childhood and her father for the first time.

In order to establish a sense of safety for herself, she told us, "I set a boundary. No more contact, including letters, phone calls. He adhered to them mostly, except that he wrote me on my birthday and at Christmas. I wrote him and told him I wanted no contact at all and since then he's cooperated. He doesn't like it, I hear through the family grapevine. But since I set a boundary, it's easier to separate and heal. He was really attached to me, more than to my siblings. I don't think I'd be as far along as I am if I hadn't separated from him completely.

I hope someday I can have a relationship with him. But if I do, he'll have to take responsibility for the things he did to me. He'll have to admit the truth."

Truth is part of the antidote for an abusive childhood. If father and daughter can admit what truly happened between them, then there is hope for reconciliation and healing. If the father refuses to acknowledge his misdeeds, his daughter can go on and travel the road to healing and growth without him.

Sometimes the truth comes out—but in a way that hurts even more. Muriel recalled the night she received a phone call that unbeknownst to her would result in a significant conversation with her father. She said, "I heard the eerie sound of my mother's voice: 'Daddy's in the hospital; he's had a major heart attack.' To be honest, I don't remember much more of the conversation, but I do know that I was having a hard time breathing, and was very cold. Somehow more calls were made, friends arrived to help me and I was soon packed to fly to California.

"Since my father was in the service, he was flown by helicopter to the nearest military base. He was in critical condition in the cardiac care unit at the hospital. He teetered between life and death for many days. A doctor had given us a bleak prognosis. The next three to four weeks were full of anxiety for us all; lots of procedures and scary moments; a lot of back and forth, to and from ICU.

"My father was very heavily medicated — understandably. He was given Valium. We all noticed his moodiness and his unfiltered thoughts. His emotions were so raw — he was constantly saying how much he loved everyone and that he was so lucky. Whatever thought arose, it was verbalized. Oftentimes we laughed hysterically or shrugged him off. Then he would obsess on the pleasure of brushing his teeth or of blowing his nose. We spent hours at his bedside, listening to him go on and on. One evening, all the relatives were away from the hospital and my dad and I had some one-on-one time.

"Daddy began telling stories — being very sentimental — often to the point of tears. He spoke of his lacrosse coach at West Point, his brother, his mother and father. It was a wonderful and tender side of my father I had never experienced. 'These were significant people.' He asked me, 'Did they realize how much I loved them?'

"Then he started speaking of Vietnam, a topic he had never shared before, at least not about what he really saw and experienced. I recall my sense of awe and disgust, as well as my desire to have my brothers nearby to hear this, too. We'd always wondered about that time of his life.

"The conversation then progressed to Daddy's immediate relationship with my mother. Daddy was so candid with me. Part of me was shocked at his ability to speak so clearly and deeply — part of me was overloaded by the content of his message. It was not new news that my parents' relationship was far from satisfactory — but as my father spoke I realized the fantasy of my parents being in love again, someday, was very far-fetched.

"My father elaborated on the bitterness and distance between him and my mother. He wept, saying he wished it had been different. He spoke freely of my mother's drinking and smoking, of her physical pains, of their dissatisfaction with the children. He seemed to repeat, 'If only I'd . . .' quite a bit.

My father felt like a failure; in his marriage, as a career person, as a father, as a citizen. He kept saying how he couldn't die now because he had to take care of my mother. Sheer determination was surely a huge part of his recovery.

"I sat there stunned and not sure how to be. My father had confided in me before, but this was so much information in one chunk and without any filters! Didn't he remember I was his daughter? I was gridlocked by my anger and my fascination — how much more would he share?

"He moved on to God and how there's a reason for having survived so many near-death moments (car accidents, dangerous military maneuvers, poor decisions, etc.). I agreed. After the few hours of listening to my father talk on and on, I was very overwhelmed.

"This is sad to me — that the one time my father really talked to someone, it was me, his daughter, it was drug-induced, and he had no memory of it.

My father taught each of us to put on a smile, no

matter how we felt. Underneath this false exterior was an underworld of pathos, despair, and love. Secret-keeping and hiding feelings are costly activities. It is no wonder my father developed a heart condition; so much emotion had been absorbed by his body."

Most of us long, if not crave, to be able to talk honestly and openly with our fathers. Sandy shared her yearning to make positive changes in her relationship with her dad, but felt unable to talk to him face-to-face. She told us, "One day I'm going to write my feelings in a letter, so he'll have time to reflect. He doesn't always do well in the moment. He can get defensive, feeling threatened and challenged. I don't think he's got the skills like we do in this generation where we process and process. My friends and I can stop each other and say, 'The way you're saying that is hurtful.' Or, 'Could you go back and discuss this again?' He doesn't have those communication tools, and I think a letter would give him more of a chance.

I may start the letter, 'You know how much I love you . . .' and then move on to say, I think we have a communication problem, give him a couple of examples, and ask him to work on it with me. I think this would be helpful. I could ask him, 'Is there anything that's bothering you about something I've done or said? I'd love to know about it, and to know what I could do. I really want to talk to you and not feel dismissed.'

"The bottom line is, life is too short. We won't be able to have conversations forever. I'm the one who will most likely to be left wishing for the conversations that will never be. I'm tired of the pattern. I'm willing to give up my alibis for why I don't call my dad, my scenario, my part of the play. I'm willing to change my script and live with the immediate, painful consequences to see a new one written that is life-giving and healthier. I want a happier, more joyful relationship with him in the long run. That's happening in other relationships in my life and I want that to happen with my dad."

Daughters aren't the only ones who long for a second chance to set things right. Bill, father of two daughters, Lisa and Kristy, expressed his regrets over past conflict. He said, "We have had our good times and our bad times. I think that when I came down with cancer in December of 1985, all of our lives were changed. I was worrying about whether they could make it in this world without me, and I became more agitated and less compassionate with them. Plus, I was going through radiation treatments and on medication, which further limited my ability to understand my daughters' wants and needs. Lisa, the older, got most of the heat because she was trying to help her younger sister. I think she felt she had to take control, but didn't realize that she was only a child herself. We had many power struggles together, and things have never been the same since.

"Lisa and Kristy are special to me in so many ways, and I hope that in spite of the past, they know that I love them both very much. They are both achievers, with a lot of love to give to people. It means so much to me to see them getting their education, and making good decisions in their lives. I heard a quotation that said children learn what unconditional love is when they have their own children, or when their parents die. I hope that, since I love my girls with all my heart, things will work themselves out someday, before time runs out for us."

No matter the disappointment, hurt, or abuse we have experienced, in our hearts we all want to be happy, at peace and reconciled with each other. The longing for reconciliation between dad and daughter can be strong, hopefully strong enough to motivate us to express difficult emotions, to finally tell the truth, and to say, "I'm sorry." It's facing the truth that precedes reconciliation, if that is to be.

Reconciliation

I've learned that life sometimes gives you a second chance.
— ANONYMOUS

People who say it cannot be done should not
interrupt those who are doing it.
— ANONYMOUS

The old adage "time heals all wounds" has proven true for some of the women we interviewed. They told us about ways their relationships with their dads have improved in time. Maybe it's because age can give daughters a new perspective. We manage our own finances and gain appreciation for the financial pressures our dads faced. We become parents and more easily identify with the struggles our parents must have gone through with us. And maybe time knocks the edges off rough spots, smoothing us both so we're not bumping up against one another like before.

Deena told us, "Now that my dad is older, he's mellowed. He's becoming the father that I always wanted him to be. During his years of alcoholism, it was awful. He was a big-time perfectionist and overachiever. This is the odd thing about my dad. Even though he was abusive in some ways, my father taught me that I was smart enough to do anything I set my mind to do. So I grew up believing I had no limitations. That's probably the greatest gift he gave me.

"Even some of his mistreatment turned out to work out for my benefit. Because of the emotional volatility that we grew up in, I learned to express my feelings and be more positive, more affectionate, more extroverted.

"Now that he's sober, he's a very different person. He says 'I love you' first now. He talks about his feelings. He's really mellowed. He's working to undo some of the damage he caused, especially with my brother, who has had the hardest time with him. I am grateful for the legacy that my dad has given me. I am very strong-willed and opinionated. My intelligence, my confidence, and my drive are all things that I have gotten from him."

Sometimes reconciliation comes along not because a father changes, but because his daughter sees him in a different light, as is the case with Desiree. Her parents were married, divorced, and remarried before she reached the age of ten. Needless to say, childhood was stressful for young Desiree. She told us, "I remember when I was five years old, my brother and I were left at a friend's house to play. I had a great time, until I found out why we were there. My mother was considering leaving my dad. My dad took us to a friend's house, knowing that she would never leave without her children. He figured this would give my mom a chance to calm down and think things over. It was the best thing

251

he could have done for the whole family. At the age of five I understood this, and didn't hold it against him.

"But later, we were forced to move. Since we had nowhere to go, Mom took us to her mother's house. Dad didn't go with us. He left for California to find work, and I hated him for that. He left Mom with five kids to raise and no support.

"Four years passed and Mom moved us to Dallas. Eventually, Dad came back to live with us again. For a while, life seemed to go well, but I still didn't trust my dad. I felt that he might leave at any moment. Well, just as I had feared, he was laid off from work and he soon left again for California. I lost all faith and trust in him. I couldn't even put the words 'love' and 'Dad' in the same sentence.

"We had to move again, and this time we went to live with my dad's mother in Odessa. After two years, Dad came back to live there with us. For a while it was tough, because each of us, in our own way, hated him. I think I detested him the most of all my siblings.

"As I passed through junior high and high school, we started doing more things together as a family. My dad enrolled in college. I thought he was crazy, way too old for college, and too self-absorbed to follow through on the course work. But he surprised me. He took a huge class load and stuck with it. I became impressed with his accomplishments, and his ability to stick it out. I began to trust him again, and we began to talk to one another.

"My graduation came and went, I got married and moved to Colorado, where I've had a long time to reflect on those times. I've had many conversations with my dad. With the help of my aunt Lynn, I've come to see that he thought he was doing his best. He's always loved us and knows he missed out on the biggest parts of our lives. Today I can honestly say that I love him and respect the fact that he never gave up on us, even when we did on him.

"Now he and I talk on a different level—about life, marriage, careers, and aspirations. Without those good and bad experiences in my life, I would be a different person than I am today. My dad showed me that whatever comes my way, deal with it the best you can and it will work out in the end. Try not to look at the world so pessimistically, but from different angles, because things aren't always what they seem at first glance. Go beyond what's given to you, because nothing is really *given* to you, it's blessed upon you."

Finding the good in our fathers is a treasure many daughters discovered as their fathers aged. Kendra told us about her precious memories of her father who had died recently of Alzheimer's. She said, "Oddly enough, I think the fact that he had that disease made him capable of showing his love. He became a little child, and I took care of him. He'd put his socks and his clothes on wrong. He also told me things he'd never said before. He'd never told me I was pretty, or he missed me, or he was glad to see me, until he had Alzheimer's. I was able to forgive so many things from the past because of how he related to me in the end.

"I'm so grateful that I could give my whole heart to him, and let go of the past. I spent hours at the nursing home, rubbing his hand, touching his leg, and talking. He'd repeat himself, but that didn't matter to me. I'd just say, 'Ah ha, ah ha.'

"Another way he tried to show amends to me was by being wonderful to my children. He was a wonderful grandfather. In fact, their favorite person was my father. He'd play cards with them, or take them to McDonald's. He did everything he never did for me, and now my children really miss him. We went to a little family reunion, and it was the first time my dad wasn't there. My daughter started crying because she used to sit by my dad. They were both introverted, so he'd been her partner to sit by at family parties. And now her grandad wasn't there."

Sometimes the longed-for reconciliation doesn't arrive until the last minute, by a bedside, saying good-bye. Kathy described her precious experience with her father; "One Thursday evening about a year ago, I held my father's hand while he died in a hospital room. It had been a day of ups and downs, with doctors shrugging their shoulders in the doorway over the relative merit of diagnostic procedures for the acute pain he was suffering. When I had walked into the room that morning to see my father moaning and my mother in tears, I knew it was going to be a long day, but I had no idea it would be the last one. I settled in to keep my mother company and help her manage the ordeal. She brightly announced my arrival to my father, who was too distracted by pain to acknowledge my presence. Once they put him on the respirator, he seemed officially out of reach.

"I was used to the hospital drill from other episodes with my father's unsteady heart. They had a way of drawing forth my most intense feelings about him. Frequently these encounters made me feel useless and invisible to him, an irritating intrusion. In a few other, and very precious, moments, I had felt he was seeing me with breathtaking clarity and responding to me with an intensity of love that fed a voracious hunger in my soul. This day, his failure to greet me reminded me of another encounter in an ICU room several years earlier. I had been sitting at his bedside, seemingly invisible to him, when his face lit up at the sight of one of his beloved students drawing the curtain aside to come deliver a card signed by the whole class. My father had lived to teach, and it had become one of my key themes to feel displaced by the way he gave his time and attention to his students rather than to his children.

"My signature hurt was triggered again that last day when the principal of the school where my father was teaching showed up for an afternoon visit, and my father rallied in welcome. By the third time I'd heard my mother marvel to the nearest hearer, "It's just remarkable the way Dave responded to Don — he opened his eyes wide, gripped his hand . . ." I was inwardly groaning at the familiar irony. 'Kathy,' I chastised myself, 'the man is seventy-five years old, and besides that he's exhausted and in pain. Why would you expect him, now, to change patterns of behavior he's spent his entire lifetime developing?' Later that day, however, I was to gain a cherished insight into my father's life that turned this irony upside down.

"In late afternoon, I left the hospital for an important personal appointment, scheduled weeks earlier. Upon my return two nurses rushed up to me, breathless with news: 'He's going down fast; there's nothing else we can do for him; your mother decided to take him off the respirator, but she's been waiting for you to come back; you'd better call your brothers.' I choked down rising sobs to wheel into action, affirming my mother's judgment and calling my brothers to set up a final phone call with their father.

"We left Dad on the respirator while we put a phone to his ear for calls with his sons. I hadn't realized he was aware of his surroundings until I saw him respond to the voice of his youngest son. Writhing with emotion, he fought to say 'I love you' through the tube that gagged him. By the time we reached my oldest brother, his struggle to communicate his love for his sons eased into a peaceful repose, as if he had received permission to die.

"Now came an interminable period of waiting for the official to arrive who was authorized to remove the respirator. 'I love you, Dad,' I said as I stroked his shoulder and my mother murmured that soon we were going to make him comfortable. Still I had no response from him, and he was more exhausted than ever. 'But Dad, you know what?' I added. 'I know you love me. I know you love me,' I said fiercely through my tears.

"In that moment my father finally acknowledged my presence — the only moment that day, the very last recognition I would ever receive from him. He thrashed against the respirator once more, unable to speak to me but visibly and intensely responding. Instantaneously it hit me that what my father most wanted on the threshold of his death was not to be reassured by hearing that I loved him, but to reassure me of his love for me — despite all his awkwardness and inadequacy in expressing it to me over the years.

"I suddenly saw my father's life as divided into two separate realms, external and internal. On the outside were those things he obviously valued, chief among them his classes, his students, the teaching methodology he was endlessly refining. But on the inside were intensities visible only when the crush of life wrung them from him, and I had been privileged to witness them. A month earlier, when he'd been hospitalized for several weeks, I had seen his face crumple in tears while I told him there was a clean slate of love for him in my heart. My father may have brightened visibly at visits from his students and colleagues, but I had never seen him weep for love of them. In those last moments he had wrestled against the restraints that bound him to reach, not his students, but his daughter.

"The mistake I had made for so many years was to

assume that only the external, visible realm defined my father's life. Because the internal one was mostly tucked away out of sight, I had assumed it simply didn't exist. But now it seemed certain that the internal realm meant more to my father than the external. Ironically, what meant the most to him was the hardest for him to express. My father had not been able to integrate very well the surface concerns of his life with what preoccupied him deep down.

"In the confusion of childhood and youth, I had felt alienated by his emotional distance. But I'd had enough signals in recent years — many of them during spontaneous visits in hospital rooms — to realize that I was firmly imbedded in his life. Now I knew how important it was to him that his daughter understand her place in his heart.

"One of the lessons I learned that day is the value of striving to live our lives in a way that reflects as much as possible what truly matters to us, what we will most urgently want to address when we realize we are up against the very last opportunity to address it. Although I still carry an unfulfilled longing for my dad's presence and attention in my life, it has been sweetened by the gifts of his love that could be unwrapped only when he left."

I'll Always Miss Him

I've learned that regardless of your relationship with your parents, you miss them terribly when they die.

— ANONYMOUS

When time runs out, we are left with our memories. If we are fortunate, we have the chance to say all we want to say, and hear all the words of love we need so that our memories comfort rather than haunt us. No matter how old daughters may become, we never outgrow our need and desire for our daddies. We'll always miss them when they are gone. Always.

Twenty-four-year-old Heather lost her father when she was only three years old. She recalled, "My dad died three days after Elvis Presley's death. I'm told that my mom and dad sorrowfully watched the events of Elvis's life shown on TV the night before.

"The next morning looked promising for another good day of wheat harvest on our Dakota farm. Grandpa thought they needed a tractor to get the new grain auger in position. But my eager, ever helpful dad said, 'No, no,' and started to push the auger toward the big grain bin. Grandpa helped. That's when the auger touched a low live wire and the sparks flew — mega volts scorching human flesh.

"Both my dad and grandpa were knocked out. When Grandpa came to, the electricity was still arcing between the auger and Dad's legs. Grandpa got a pole and rolled

Dad away and called Grandma to come help. She came running, but all her rescue training was futile as she tried to breathe life into her dear son. She told me that she paused for a few seconds. It was so quiet that she could almost hear the angels whisking my dad away. He was only twenty-three.

"When I was told that Daddy had gone to Heaven and wouldn't be home again, I stamped my foot and cried, 'Well, why didn't he stop by and get us and take us with him?' I kept asking my mom if he needed his clothes that were still in the closet.

"When it used to thunder, I'd ask, 'Is Daddy bowling up there in heaven? Does God have a bowling ball too?' That ingrained thought took away my fear of thunderstorms, lasting all my life. I'd beg, 'Couldn't we please, just for a weekend, go to Heaven and see Daddy?' Looking back I can see what I put my poor mother through.

"I look like him — red hair, freckles, fine features. Grandpa used to tell me, if I'd been a boy, they would have put overalls on me and it'd be like having his boy back again. I can live with that. I was so young when he died that I treasure the few memories I have. I remember rides with my dad on the tractor. My daddy's arm muscles bulged as he powered the giant piece of machinery. I felt so important sitting by his side with my hands hanging onto the steering wheel. My younger sister, who was only three months old when he died, has no such memories. Yet we both wish, if not yearn, for our dad. My mom has since remarried and we've adjusted well.

It's taken me a long time to get to this place of acceptance. At least I feel healed."

Losing a father at an early age can have a powerful impact on a young girl. Gloria told us that her father died when she was only sixteen years old. She said, "Because he died when I was so young, I have very few memories. Even though my father's been dead since 1969, to this day, he still has an impact on me. My husband says people have guardian angels, and I believe my father's my guardian angel. Every time something important happens, I still think about him.

"In 1976, when my daughter was born, I wished he were there. My father had very distinguished-type cheeks on his face, and when I first saw my daughter she had his cheekbones. Instantly I missed him."

Perhaps those who lose their fathers when they are still girls have a special challenge, that of getting "stuck" in the grief, in their need for a daddy to help guide them into womanhood. Alice was almost grown—she was nineteen—when her father died. But she found it hard to move on with her life. She told us, "When I was a little girl, my dad and I would walk along the Oregon beach. He had big hands, so I would hold his index finger. We would watch the waves, our bare feet in the sand. That's how I remember him. Standing there with me on the beach.

"When I was nineteen, he had a heart attack and was in the hospital for ten days. The doctors released him and he died within three hours of coming home. When he was in the hospital, I made it a point of not saying good-bye. But as I left the last day he was in the hospital, I turned around and said, 'Good-bye.' I'm so glad I did that. Later, I realized it was some kind of premonition.

"I was at work when they told me he died. I had so many conflicting emotions — anger, confusion, grief. I would go to the beach and walk and walk. Several times I went to the cemetery. I couldn't seem to get past my sadness, my loss. Then one day, I could almost hear my dad say, 'Get out of here. Get on with your life.' I felt that he didn't want me to live in mourning or anger any longer. That helped me move on. I still treasure him in my heart, but I feel free to live, not dwell on his death."

No matter when our fathers die, it seems too soon. Dottie was thirty when her father passed away. She told us, "I felt loved by my father all my life. My dad was sick a lot when I was a little girl. He had tuberculosis and was in the hospital for a year and a half, so I didn't see him. When he was there, I wrote him a letter and I signed it 'your favorite daughter.' He had two daughters, but I wanted to be the favorite, and he used to joke around for years that I was his favorite daughter. If I would call after I got married and moved out, my mom would tell him that 'your favorite daughter called.' I don't think that she would do this in front of my sister, because she thought she was the favorite, too.

"I was eleven when I wrote that letter to my dad, and thirty when he died. When I went to the nursing home to get his effects, they wanted me to go through his wallet, because there was no I.D. in it. I went through it and the only thing that was in it was my letter; he had kept that for almost twenty years."

When we interviewed Rita the loss of her father was relatively new, having buried him two years previously. She told us, "My dad lived with me for many years. He was diabetic and had a mind of his own about medication. Every morning I would have to check his urine specimen. I would dip the little stick in the urine, since he'd lie to me and get into the cookie jars and stuff like that.

"One morning, about ten years ago, when my daughter was about twenty-one but still living at home, he put apple juice in his specimen glass. Then he woke up my daughter and he asked her to test it. She said, 'No, Mom has to do this.' He said, 'No, I want you to do this, test it for me.' So, she went and got the sticks and before she dipped one, he said, 'Oh, wait a minute, there's too much in there,' and he drank half of it!

"My daughter went crazy. I was asleep and I woke up to her screaming and running up and down the hall. She couldn't even talk to me and she kept screaming and gagging. My father was in the bathroom, probably eighty-five at the time, laughing and laughing. He was just a fun, crazy man.

"He had such a weird sense of humor, and we loved him dearly. We have a million stories. Toward the end, it got really tough taking care of him, because he was a man and I had to bathe him. I would leave his underwear on and I would wear my shorts and top and get in the shower with him. He'd say, 'Don't look at me!' and I'd say, 'I'm not going to look at you,' and then I'd scrub him. He told me I was scrubbing him like he was a dog. We laughed so much in that shower.

"Then finally, they had to amputate his leg, because of the diabetes, and I had to put him in a nursing facility. Even then, we had so much fun. He loved to take his prosthesis off and do this little can-can with his stump. He would do this for the grandkids while singing. I would take him for walks and tell him I was going to hang this sign and put him on the corner of Beach Boulevard and say I WORK FOR FOOD. I said, 'We could make a lot of money, Dad.' He might have actually gone with it. He was so game for anything.

"He taught me to be an optimist. He was happy and I think a little crazy. Like him, I tend to play tricks on people. I knew he loved me. He was always on my side. He was just wonderful. I miss him very, very much."

EPILOGUE

Legacy of Love: What I Want the World to Know About My Dad

No matter what, I'm daddy's little girl. Even though I have sort of a boyfriend and am almost in middle school, I'm still his little girl. I'll always love him the same — and he me. Even though I'm too big to carry, I'm not too big to hug him. If I'm too big to play Candy Land with him, I'm not too big for tic-tac-toe. No matter what happens, I'll love him forever. I'll always be daddy's little girl.

— LYNDSAY LEIGH BROOKS, DAUGHTER OF MARK BROOKS,
1995 PGA CHAMPION

From our fathers we receive a legacy, first of life, and then of love. This legacy passes from one generation to the next, from our fathers to us, and then from us to our children.

What do you want the world to know about *your* dad? If you had the chance to describe the legacy you've received from your father, what would *you* say? Here are what a few daughters told us in response to our question:

DEBBY HALVERSON MARKEY, daughter of Dr. Richard Halverson, former chaplain of the United States Senate
My dad served as chaplain to the Senate from 1978 until 1995. He died in November 1996. His only formal-

ized task was to open the Senate with prayer each session. But my father expanded his role immensely. He was Everyman to every man, believing that he was to care for all people who were involved in the Senate, regardless of stature or station. From doorman to senator, he treated them all with the same dignity and care.

My dad spent his days loving people because he believed that was his 'job' as a Christian. After he opened the Senate with prayer, he'd go into the press room and chat with several members of the press. Then he'd walk through the leadership offices to say hello to the staff. Each morning, he'd go into the dining room and sing to the waitresses. Once a week, he made it a practice to have coffee with all the police who patrolled the buildings, as well as hosting a coffee with the pages and cloakroom personnel.

I guess you could describe my dad as a "hugger." He hugged everybody. He loved to say, "I am the servant of the servants of The Servant." People fell in love with my dad, regardless of their religious background, because he didn't try to convert or change anyone. He just loved them, so they naturally loved him back. People respond to authentic love, while they'll reject religious hypocrisy. Dad tried to dissuade the church from being preoccupied with political agendas and to make a statement by living life fully in the present, with compassion and acceptance. When it's all said and done, that's what I want the world to know about my dad—that he really knew the true meaning of God's love and tried his best to live it every day.

CINDY MORGAN, Word Records recording artist,
daughter of Cova Morgan

Even though my dad was a mechanic, he dreamed of being a songwriter. He took a day off from work to go to Nashville, hoping to get someone to listen to his songs. The people at RCA agreed to meet with him and really liked one of his songs. In fact, they asked him to stay overnight so he could hang out at the Grand Ole Opry and then play his song for their publisher.

He told RCA that he'd promised his family he'd be back that night and be at work the next day. These people said, 'Well, if you wanna be in country music you have to be in Nashville.' Nashville was three hours away from where we lived in Harrogatte, Tennessee, and he felt like his absence would be too hard on his family emotionally and financially. So for the next twenty years he devoted his life to his family and returned to work as a VW mechanic.

He never made us feel guilty for his decision, or that somehow he'd missed out on life because of us. Instead, he showered us with love. He would come in to my room in the morning to wake me up by putting a warm washcloth on my head and ask, "Do you have anything I can iron for you?" My dad truly loved giving more than receiving. He would even help me do dishes, which I hated. How many dads are like that?

I went on to pursue my dream of singing, and landed a contract with Word Records. Two years ago I found a cassette of my mom singing a song my dad had written when I was a little girl, about twenty years ago. My guitar player and I took the lyrics and rewrote the music. Believe it or not, his song became number one on the charts for Contemporary Christian Music! The American Society of Composers and Performers inducted my dad into the Number One Club, for all songwriters whose songs have gone to number one on the *Billboard* magazine charts. He got a Number One Club jacket, a plaque, and a special ceremony — all on his first published song. To add to that, he has been nominated as 1997 Songwriter of the Year for the Gospel Music Association's Dove Awards.

I know what it is like to have a dream for music, and my dad had that same dream. He gave up his dreams so that my dreams could come true — that's what I want the world to know about my dad.

JOANNE DEALEY, president/owner of MD&A Advertising Company, daughter of Stan Grzywacz

My father was born in East St. Louis and made his way in life alone, losing both of his parents before reaching the age of fourteen. For the most part, he was a tough guy — strong-willed, opinionated, and unbending. But there was more to him than this.

• He loved to sing in the car and eat ham sandwiches on the roadside in New Mexico.

- He thought you could tell more about a man on the golf course than in the board room.
- He believed a real gentleman should own a tuxedo and know how to dance.
- He read the newspaper every day and expected us to do the same.
- He loved baseball. I have never been to a game without remembering his description of the way grass smells in a ballpark.
- We had dinner every night at exactly 6:00 P.M.
- No boys called our house after ten.
- We discussed everything in plain terms, even 'parking,' which he thought was 'foolish.' He told us any kissing that couldn't be done on his own couch shouldn't be done at all.
- He loved God, but he was scared of Baptists.
- He thought my mom was beautiful.

Even though we lived in a small town in West Texas, he was the first to remind us that the world was a big and wonderful place. He'd say, "Everyone out there gets up in the morning and puts their pants on one leg at a time," so I grew up believing I could do anything I wanted to do, and that I was as good as anyone else. I naturally understood my obligation to make the world a little bit more wonderful than it was before I got there.

Even though my dad's been dead for thirteen years, I still have the urge to pick up the phone and tell him I've been thinking about him today. I remember when I moved out on my own he told me, "Everything between you and me is just like everything between you and God. I will never stop loving you, no matter how far away you might need to go." And I did go far, I left Lubbock, Texas, after graduating from college and moved to New York City to work with a major advertising agency.

He encouraged me with common sense advice. He said, "Keep this dime in your pocket and remember the things you really need are already in your backyard. Don't forget your dictionary, and your Bible should be frayed." My dad exhibited enormous courage and inspired it in other people, by using the context of the everyday. That's what I want the world to know about my dad.

IRENE FLORES, stylist and skin specialist, daughter of Lawrence Banuelos

I remember my father as the embodiment of life itself! He may have been poor in the financial sense, being a Mexican-American farm laborer in northern California, but he was rich in self esteem, talent, and a robust enjoyment for living.

He worked hard. We all did. I remember one summer he packed us all up and we traveled across the valley to pick plums for one of the growers. We lived in a shack in the groves, and my mother literally hosed it down before we moved in to clean out the dirt. The owner asked my dad, "How many workers do you have?" My dad said, "Don't you worry about it. I'll take care of everything." The owner asked, "But when will you have the fruit picked?" My dad repeated, "Don't you worry about it. I'll take care of everything." And he did.

He and my mother got me and my three sisters up before dawn so we would be dressed, fed, and ready to start picking by sunup. With the first hint of sunlight, we went to the fields and worked steadily until the middle of the afternoon. The owner was amazed at how thoroughly we harvested his crop, and with our handling of the fruit, he got the best price possible. The next summer, the owner built us a new house to live in. That's the way my dad did things, and that's how he taught us to work.

When he wasn't working, he was making music. He played several instruments—the trombone, the sax, the clarinet. I grew up with singing and dancing and music in the house. We were rich in rhythm, warmth, and passion.

When I was eighteen, I met a man named Joseph who was visiting from southern California. I adored Joe, but wanted my dad's approval. I overheard Dad say to Mom, "Joe is the first real man Irene's brought home." I knew then that Joe was the man for me. We married within the year. I didn't realize it then, but Joe is so much like my father—a musician, true to his word, a genuinely good man who has stuck with me through the ups and downs of our married life.

Joe and I moved to southern California. We had two sons, Thomas and Timothy. When Tom was just two years old, we went up north to visit my parents. Dad took Tom to town one afternoon. As they walked across the street, a car careened around the corner and the driver didn't see them. At the last minute, my dad looked up and saw the car bearing down on them. With no time to get out of the way, my dad calmly moved Tom behind him and took the full blow of the car's impact. Both my dad and Tom were thrown some fifty feet. Tom had two little scratches on his face. My father was dead.

When Tom was old enough, he learned that his grandfather had given his life for him. He vowed that because of his grandfather's sacrifice, he would make something of his life. Even though I was born the daughter of a poor migrant worker, my son Tom has a master's degree from the University of Southern California and is a successful businessman. Admittance into USC is difficult, and it was even harder on us as a family to pay his tuition. But we were all committed to the same goal. We are equally committed to helping our other son, Tim, reach his professional goals as well.

I want the world to know that my dad was full of life, to the very end. And even in his death, he passed on a passion for learning, accomplishment, and living life fully to me, my husband, and my children. He had a funny little way he'd wiggle his hips when he danced. And now, Tom's one-and-a-half-year-old daughter dances the very same way. My dad's spirit is alive and well in his children, grandchildren, and even his great-grandchildren. I'm proud to be his daughter, and I believe that somehow, somewhere he knows it.

LYNN BARRINGTON, co-author,
daughter of Jeff Benney Bowden

My dad may have gotten up to a sixth grade education. No one will ever know for sure because the story would change depending on the point my dad was trying to make at the time. If he wanted you to feel better about him, it was the sixth grade; if he was trying to encourage me about education, it was the fourth. Either way, it wasn't much education.

He loved to tell me how he walked to school in the snow with holes in his shoes. It was amazing how the story would come in handy when I was whining about something I wanted. He left school when he was probably around eleven or twelve and went out to work in the oil fields by lying about his age. Back in those days you could work for hire if you were fourteen. Once he started working, he never left the oil fields. He became a real expert. In fact, there's probably not a major oil company who hasn't hired him to come in and troubleshoot a bad well at some time or another. He was on call twenty-four hours a day. He would work away from home for a week or ten days at a time. Then he'd come home for a few days, have business meetings at the office, and go back out into the field. He was a hard worker.

He had one of the first mobile phones. At that time, you had to go through a mobile-phone operator for each call and the reception was quite poor. I remember he used to carry a set of phone books in his car that I would get to sit on and be just as tall as my brothers in the backseat. I was so proud to be one of the few girls whose dad had a phone in his car.

Even though he had the mobile phone, he worked in horrible conditions to make sure that we lived an upper-middle-class lifestyle. He'd have to stay days at a time in a trailer that consisted of a bed, bathroom, and kitchenette. The trailer was filthy because the oil field hands would come in and have coffee with him to get out of the cold. It smelled like oil, dirt, and grime. Even the interior of his car smelled like those oil fields. But he didn't complain; rather, he made it seem like a treat when my mom and I would load up and take him hot food and spend the night. He would play cards and dominoes with me in that stinky trailer. I didn't care how it smelled, though, because I was with my daddy. He always had a joke or good story. I laughed a lot with my daddy.

My father now suffers from Alzheimer's. He is in the fifth stage of this progressive disease and even though his physical health is good, he hasn't known who I am for almost two years. He is no longer able to communicate. He mumbles and makes up sounds. My stepmother takes really wonderful care of him. She has been dedicated to him, and I will always be thankful for that. Sometimes he doesn't know who she is either. It's a very sad disease.

Recently, my friend Fred asked me what I think an Alzheimer's patient feels or knows when they are that far gone. I don't know, of course, but I wonder about my dad every day in that context. I hope he is at peace inside and that he isn't aware of what is happening. He was such a brilliant man and came so far in life for the little education he had. I comfort myself in the knowledge that before he was diagnosed, he and I were at peace.

We had quite the up-and-down relationship, but it was out of our great love for each other and freedom to get mad at each other. Now I know that I wasted time by how I handled my anger. I learned when you reconcile, the gray cloud leaves. I learned this the hard way, and waited far too long to work things out with my dad. We only had a few months before he was diagnosed of genuine reconciliaion. He knew that I loved him madly, and I knew he loved me madly. We both trusted that in the end, and we reconciled. We both said everything we needed to say to each other, and that means a lot now that he can't understand a word I say, or vice versa.

I want the world to know that my dad is a good man, a fun guy. With almost no education and great love for his family, he raised three children who all have college degrees, who are living good lives and affecting the world in a positive way. I told him, before his mind started to go, that I would make him proud. He will never get to read this book, with these incredible stories of daddies and daughters collected from around our country, but I know, Daddy, this would have made you proud.

CARMEN RENEE BERRY, co-author
daughter of Dr. David A. Berry

My dad found me crying in my bedroom after the first day of class, my senior year in high school. I hated school, but I knew that I had to go to repeat junior calculus. From grade school, I'd been in the mentally gifted program and was used to getting A's and B's in my classes. But during my junior year, I took an advanced calculus class in which the teacher decided to grade on the curve. This meant that some of us would have to fail.

The end of my junior year, my report card had a D next to calculus, a grade I had never had before. My parents were very upset and my father told me that I'd have to take the class over and raise my grade. All summer long I dreaded returning to school. When the day came, all I could do was cry.

When my dad found out why I was sobbing, he said something remarkable to me. He said, "You are more important to me than a grade. You have outgrown high school and need new experiences, so forget repeating calculus. For me to make you do that would simply be a matter of pride. I'll do what I can to help you graduate early." If I'd ever doubted it before, I knew for sure that day that my dad had his own way of living life, full of grace. He believed there were many ways of getting to a goal, and saw possibilities where others might have seen only one way. He passed that on to me.

When it was time for me to go to college, I wanted to have adventures. My parents, of course, expected me to get an education. So we came up with a plan. As long as I would stay in school, I could change schools every semester and see the world. Over the next few years, I earned a bachelor's degree and two master's degrees — and have transcripts at a total of ten colleges and universities. I also traveled around the world at the same time. He knew that a real education was more than what was written in books, and he supported, and financed, a truly unique education for his daughter.

While my dad held traditional values of accomplishment, he had his own ideas about how to reach those goals. And he didn't seem to care what other people thought about his unconventional ways. Long before feminism was a major influence, my father always let me know that my being female was in no way a barrier to achieving whatever I wanted. Fathers today may raise their daughters to be independent, but I grew up in the fifties. Even then, my dad had his own ideas about how to raise a daughter. When I was around six, we made a go-cart together. We made it out of old crates; we sawed the wood, nailed it together, put wheels on it with a steering rope. It even had brakes. I thought it was so cool!

As I grew up, my dad and I made a lot of other things together — a crystal radio, a rock polisher for my rock collection, even an electric guitar. At Christmas, my mom would give me dolls and tea sets, and my dad would get me things like erector sets, chemistry sets, or train sets. Both of my parents created in me the belief that I could do whatever I put my mind to.

This sense of confidence has gotten me through situations that others with a bit more sense might have shied away from. But I have just kept on going, sort of like the energizer bunny. As anyone knows who follows a dream, at first it can be hard to tell anyone about it. I felt foolish telling people I wanted to be a writer. When you haven't published anything, it can be intimidating to say your dream out loud. But I could always talk to my dad about my dreams. Knowing he would support me was part of the fabric of my life. I knew he'd never make me feel foolish. Instead, he'd encourage me, reminding me of my various talents. He made me feel the sky was the limit.

With his encouragement, I kept at my dream to write —year after year, rejection letter after rejection letter— until finally I got my big break and signed my first contract. His support played a big part in my endurance, and I share my success with him as well.

The timing of this book, *Daddies and Daughters*, can only be a gift from God. When Lynn Barrington, my co-author, first shared with me her idea of writing a book celebrating the bond between daughters and fathers, I was excited and thought it would be relatively easy to write. I remember calling my parents last July 11th, telling them that we had just landed a wonderful contract with Simon & Schuster. Little did I know then what was ahead for us.

Before we started writing the manuscript, everything changed. On October 13, Lynn and I went out to dinner to discuss the book. When I returned home, I listened to

278

my messages and heard my mother's strained voice telling me, "Carmen, your father's had an accident. We're at the emergency room." I called Lynn, who had just gotten home, and the two of us raced to the hospital.

Parts of that evening I still can't recall, because seeing my father in that condition was so traumatic. That was the first of many nights my mother, our very supportive friends, and I spent at the hospital fighting for his life.

From October to February, I saw my father overcome enormous physical challenges — he endured plastic surgery, the attachment of a "halo" (a very nice word for a horrible-looking contraption that is literally screwed several places into the skull), surgery to set his leg . . . and then, when it was time, the reversal of all these procedures. In addition to the initial injuries, he contracted and overcame pneumonia. It took a strong will to deal with this series of traumatic events. Through it all, my father kept his sense of humor, his stamina, and a faith in God I'd seen him exhibit throughout his life. And he continued to do things in his own unique way.

Over the Christmas holidays, my mother and I attempted to care for him at home. He spent a week at their home in West Covina, California, and then we moved him to my place in Pasadena. As his situation deteriorated, we realized that he needed more care than we could give, but I hated the idea of putting him in a nursing home. The day we decided he needed to go to a nursing home, I sobbed and sobbed. I was sure he would be very upset about the decision. As they wheeled him out to the van, he looked back at me and the home nurse and said, waving, "Thanks a lot, folks. I'm out of here." I knew then that my father was still in charge of his own life.

After suffering a number of strokes, I believe he knew more about what was going on than he was able to express. He would try to talk to us and the words were often jumbled, but when we looked each other in the eyes, I had the sense that he really did know what was going on. Even though we had struggled against the odds for the last four months, I never believed that he would actually die. But a week and a half ago, for the first time, I could envision us at his funeral. I believe that God was preparing me for what was ahead, and that my father had decided he did not want to live a life unable to communicate, unable to work with his hands, unable to teach.

Just four days after the doctors had removed the final apparatus and had told us he was healed of all the injuries from the accident, he died. A day or so ago someone asked me if my dad had given up. To that I have to answer, no. My father never gave up. He survived the poor hospital care, the many surgeries, the moves from facility to facility (where he always announced that he was in charge), and then, having accomplished all that, he made the decision to die the same way he lived—on his own terms. In his own way, he told us, "Thanks a lot, folks. I'm out of here."

Daddies and Daughters, was not as easy to write as I

had first imagined. In fact, it was quite difficult writing about fathers when mine was suffering so, to recall childhood memories when my dad couldn't remember my name. But then, I can think of no more rewarding task than to tell the world that I love my daddy. Not only that, I respect and admire him. This books is dedicated to his memory, a tribute to a dad named David Berry, who loved his daughter well, and who will never be forgotten.

About the Authors

Carmen Renee Berry, the coauthor of the *New York Times* best-seller *Girlfriends: Invisible Bonds, Enduring Ties*, is a former psychotherapist and now a nationally certified massage and body worker. She holds an M.S.W. from the University of Southern California and a master's degree in social sciences from the University of Northern Arizona. *Daddies and Daughters* is her eleventh book; other books include the best-selling *When Helping You Is Hurting Me, Coming Home to Your Body, Is Your Body Trying to Tell You Something*, and *Girlfriends Talk About Men*. She lives in Pasadena, California, with three cats: Sassy, Stud, and Sweet Pea.

Lynn Barrington is president of 4552 Entertainment Street, a music publishing and production company. She has been the director of publishing for several different record labels and has worked as well in various capacities for MGM, Twentieth Century Fox, and Universal Studios. Lynn has a bachelor's degree in music education from Oklahoma Baptist University. While living in Arlington, Texas, she enjoys golf, playing with her dog, Otto, and a good stiff Diet Coke.